Deep Country

Five Years in the Welsh Hills

NEIL ANSELL

PENGUIN BOOKS

PENGUIN BOOKS

Published by the Penguin Group
Penguin Books Ltd, 80 Strand, London wc2r orl, England
Penguin Group (USA) Inc., 375 Hudson Street, New York, New York 10014, USA
Penguin Group (Canada), 90 Eglinton Avenue East, Suite 700, Toronto, Ontario, Canada m4p 2y3
(a division of Pearson Penguin Canada Inc.)
Penguin Ireland, 25 St Stephen's Green, Dublin 2, Ireland (a division of Penguin Books Ltd)
Penguin Group (Australia), 250 Camberwell Road, Camberwell, Victoria 3124, Australia
(a division of Pearson Australia Group Pty Ltd)
Penguin Books India Pvt Ltd, 11 Community Centre, Panchsheel Park, New Delhi – 110 017, India
Penguin Group (NZ), 67 Apollo Drive, Rosedale, Auckland 0632, New Zealand
(a division of Pearson New Zealand Ltd)
Penguin Books (South Africa) (Pty) Ltd, 24 Sturdee Avenue,
Rosebank, Johannesburg 2196, South Africa

Penguin Books Ltd, Registered Offices: 80 Strand, London wc2r orl, England

www.penguin.com

First published by Hamish Hamilton 2011
Published in Penguin Books 2012
002

Copyright © Neil Ansell, 2011
All rights reserved

The moral right of the author has been asserted

Map by Andrew Farmer

Typeset by Palimpsest Book Production Limited, Falkirk, Stirlingshire
Printed in Great Britain by Clays Ltd, St Ives plc

ISBN: 978-0-141-04932-8

www.greenpenguin.co.uk

ALWAYS LEARNING   **PEARSON**

Contents

Prologue

The drivers always seem bemused when I tell them where to drop me. On a long, fast sweep of the road flanked with serried ranks of pine, there is a track through the woods, but it is invisible to anyone who doesn't know exactly where to look. It is the merest whisper of a trail; I doubt that anyone other than me has trodden it for many a year. I step into the cool hush of the pine forest and make my way down to the valley floor. Through the trunks I can see the glimmer of light on water far below. Way above me a sparrowhawk is circling in her display flight.

There is a footbridge over the river, an old suspension bridge, and I pause midway to lean on the rail and look downriver at the water boiling over submerged rocks and veering around little mossy islands. The hours I have spent watching this river roll by, sometimes at a crawl, sometimes in a raging brown torrent. And then I look up; the day is wearing on and I still have a mountainside to climb. The steepest of steep fields, if you stretch your arms out in front of you as you are walking up it you can almost touch the ground ahead of you. It is May and the field is a haze of blue, the air thick with scent. Bluebells are flowers of the forest, not the field, but long, long ago this field was wooded; the biggest stumps, those too big to be dragged out by tractor, still stud the ground. And the bluebells still emerge in their thousands every spring in remembrance; the ground layer of the ghost of a wood.

Over a crumbling gate is the moor. The tight coils of bracken are unfurling, the whole hillside is bursting into life. Before long the bracken will be head-high and the trail will be a green tunnel. A pair of red kites circles lazily above the valley, and a solitary raven flies straight and determined above the fields below me, cronking as he sees me. I follow his course; I know exactly where he is headed. The liquid, bubbling call of a curlew trickles down the mountainside. The hills are calling; they always call me back.

Unless you know where to look the cottage is singularly hard to find, and that's the way I like it. I reach it just before nightfall and kick open the back door; this is the only way to open it. I don't have long before dark, and there is plenty to do while there is still enough light to see by. I must fetch in water, bring in logs from the woodshed, and fill the lamps. I must get the fire lit and make up a bed, and hang a kettle of water for cooking dinner. Then I'll sit out front with a cup of tea, look out at the view as the sun sets, and count the bats out of the loft. It's good to be back.

There are some mornings here when I could be on an island. In the night the valley fills with fog, in the darkness I can just make out a snake of it settling on the valley floor, following every twist and turn of the river. But when I wake the sunshine is streaming in through the curtains and I throw them aside to look out across a sea of foam. Here, at a thousand feet, it rarely reaches me. The tops of the nearest trees emerge like mangroves but beyond that it is twenty miles to the nearest dry land, the looming whale-backs of the Black Mountains and the spires of the Brecon Beacons. Sometimes the fog is so thick that when I step outside it laps at my feet in waves, and if I walk a few paces downhill I can barely see my hands. And then as the sun rises higher it starts to burn away, the tide turns and the fog retreats down-valley, leaving a hillside glistening with dew.

Morning comes, and I am alone but not alone. There is a redstart on the wire and a wagtail bobbing on the roof. Blackbirds are nesting in the woodshed, on an upturned hoe hanging from a nail on the wall. The redstarts seem to be nesting in the gables, they must approve of the new roof. Their nesting box they have surrendered to the great tits; when I open the lid eight hungry mouths gape up at me. After a few seconds, four of the baby birds slump back down, but the hungry ones keep pushing up, refusing to accept that I have nothing for them. The hole in the ash out front, which becomes home for some bird or another every year, has been occupied by a shy pair of stock doves; it is finally their turn. In the early-morning sun they display together in celebration, launching themselves from their nesting tree, and flying in a tight circle together, so close they are almost touching. The lead bird holds a little twig in its beak, as if it is returning to the ark.

I sit in my front porch looking way down across the valley to the faraway hills while sharpening my saw. Twenty-one strokes to the right, and twenty-one strokes to the left. There has been a dry spell, so it makes good sense to saw as many logs as possible while I am here, to split them and shed them before they have a chance to get wet. With the weather here so unpredictable it is reassuring to have several weeks' wood in reserve in the woodshed; a backlog. As I sit preparing my chainsaw I see that the swallows have built their nest in the porch; I reach in and run my finger around the smooth mud lining. There is a single egg, she has laid her first today. She will lay another egg each day until the clutch is complete and she can start to incubate; then it will be time to abandon my porch to the swallows, and just use the back door.

I was always surprised by the number of birds that chose to nest in close proximity to the cottage when I lived here full-time; now the place is even less disturbed there are more than ever before. For the very first time, a pair of goldfinches is nesting in the garden. It takes me a while to find the nest in the blackthorns just inside the gate where the chaffinches sometimes make their home. The gold-finches are delightful little birds with cherry-red faces and brilliant golden bars on their wings. The nest is far from the trunk as is their habit, where it will be tossed about in the breeze, but the little mossy cup is built so deep that it will not be upset by even the wildest wind. The nest is about two metres up, too high to inspect, so I hold up a mirror over it to see the four tiny eggs nestled within.

I have picked a fine time for a visit; the spring evening is as balmy as any summer's night. Tomorrow, if the weather holds, I shall head for the hills. As darkness begins to settle lightly on the land, a falcon appears over the front field. Birds of prey can be hard to tell apart on the wing, but not this one. I have it pinned immediately as a hobby, from its arc, its spirit. It is far from its usual haunts; even after all these years, the place can still bring me surprises. The falcon doesn't seem to be hunting, more just celebrating life. As night falls, I watch enraptured as it swoops and banks and swerves on its scimitar wings, until I can see it no more. Never before have I seen a bird that looked so like it was dancing in the air.

The grass in the garden, fenced off from the sheep, has grown tall and rank in the months since I was last here. I can barely make out the shape of where my vegetable beds used to lie. I would cut it back were it not for the hares. Hares are the hardiest of creatures; they live out in the fields all year long and can breed at any time of the year. But this year they have chosen the spring, and have chosen my garden. There are two leverets now grazing just a few feet away in the lush grass of the fertile soil where my vegetables once grew. They are almost the size of rabbits, and must already be weaned as the jill is leaving them largely to their own devices; I have only seen her once. The two little hares watch me watching them but don't seem to mind me so long as I keep my eyes fixed on them. If I glance away for a moment they seem to just melt away into the long grass.

I lived alone in this cottage for five years, summer and winter, with no transport, no phone. This is the story of those five years, where I lived and how I lived. It is the story of what it means to live in a place so remote that you may not see another soul for weeks on end. And it is the story of the hidden places that I came to call my own, and the wild creatures that became my society.

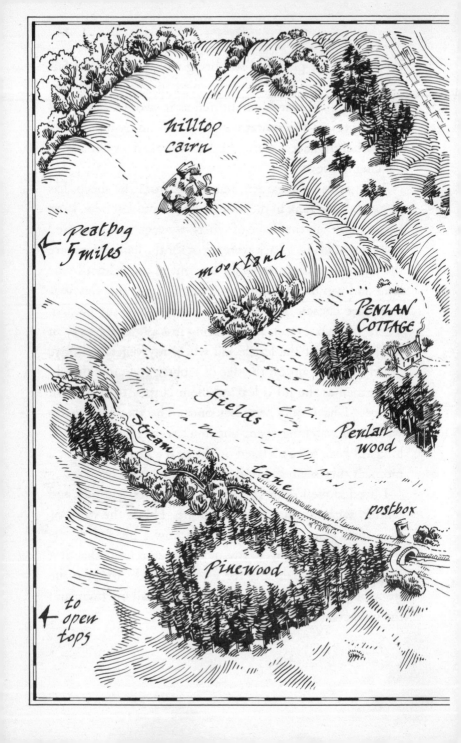

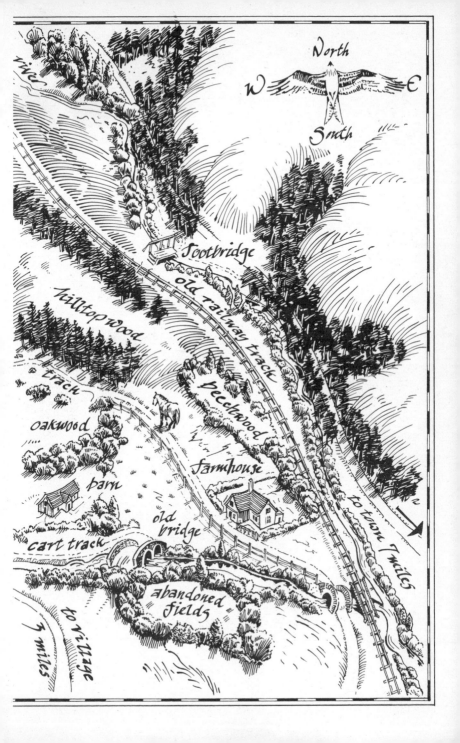

1. *The Empty Quarter*

I first came to the cottage on an autumn night the year of my thirtieth birthday, setting off at four in the afternoon from London straight after working a double shift. I hadn't expected to make it that night, and had arranged to stop over with friends in Swindon and continue my journey in the morning. But the first truck that picked me up from the start of the M4 took me clear through to Leigh Delamere Services, so I decided to press on. Things slowed down after that as the roads got less and less busy. I was dropped off at midnight in the village by the last lorry driver of the day, said my thanks and got out my hand-drawn map. I took the bridge across the river, then headed into the lanes. The cottage is three miles from the village, along lanes that get progressively narrower and steeper and finally give way to a dirt track. As I walked, tawny owls called my way, the *too-whit* of the females, the *too-whoo* of the males. I counted five territories, it felt as though I was being handed from one to the next like a baton in a relay race. There was no moon but the Milky Way was a bright smear across the sky. From the last farmhouse there were seven gates to open and close, and I followed the track rather than cut across the fields even though it was so steep the trail wound drunkenly back and forth.

Although later I would prefer to take my night walks by starlight alone, everything was new to me then and I carried a torch. Everywhere it shone, eyes were reflected back at me; there were rabbits lined up along the edges of every field. I didn't know it then, but they were at their peak. Soon, myxomatosis would hit again, and the population would crash to almost nothing, before slowly beginning to rise again. Although if you know where to look you can see the cottage like a beacon on the hillside from the main road ten or fifteen miles south, once you leave the village the lay of the land makes it disappear from view until you have closed the last gate, turned the last corner, and the track finally levels off. And there it was that I caught my first glimpse of Penlan Cottage, nestled against the hillside, surrounded by a ring of ash trees. After the steep trek into the darkness of the mountains it was a welcome sight. It looked like home.

From its northern aspect at least, the cottage looked like a child's drawing of a house; four square windows, a central door, a steeply pitched roof, a tall smoking chimney stack and a tree to either side. From the south, it looked more like a shed, as it had been weatherproofed with corrugated-iron cladding and painted cream. It looked bad, but was probably necessary, for it was so exposed to the elements. A friend once described it as the only place he had ever been where it rained uphill. There was a porch too, a slab of stone, a timber frame clad again with corrugated-iron sheeting. This was a fine place to sit and look out across the valley, and when it was wet the rain would clatter on the metal roof like gunshot. Beside the porch was a sprawling cotoneaster, and I would transplant a wild honeysuckle from the woods which would grow to drape over the entire porch and fill it with a nectar that would attract hawkmoths, including sometimes the elephant hawkmoth, in pastel pink and mossy green, to my eyes more beautiful than any of the butterflies we have here in Britain. There were two windows facing south, from the living room and the main bedroom above, and the stone walls were sufficiently thick that the sills inside were deep enough to sit in should the weather drive me in from the porch. It was a view that never ceased to draw the eye. Either side of the house there was a single narrow slotted window. The place was a Victorian gamekeeper's cottage, and these windows were designed for keeping an eye on the pheasant pens on each side of the building. The one to the west looked out across the moors. You could cross two fields and you were on open moorland; you could walk west for twenty miles without seeing another house, or a road, or a fence. This uninhabited swathe of the Cambrian Mountains right in the very heart of the country has been called the green desert of Wales, its empty quarter.

Just downhill across the track there was once a farmhouse, presumably Penlan Farm. An overgrown rocky mound in the approximate shape of a large building from which now sprout full-grown ash trees, it is not so much a ruin as the ghost of another era. This landscape is far wilder than it once was; the hundred-and-twenty-acre hill farm around me now barely supported a single elderly tenant farmer, yet scattered around its fields were the remains of five farmhouses or labourers' cottages, and a mill. With mechanization came massive depopulation, as people moved first south to the mines, and then much later to the cities of the South Wales coast, and further. The world may be filling with people, but there are still a few places that buck the trend and are being left behind, abandoned by the gathering crowds.

The cottage had been built out of rocks scavenged from the ruins of the farmhouse, and placed back in the quarry from which they were excavated. Penlan was tucked into this scallop that had been scooped out of the steep hillside, the rock wall behind it was as high as the guttering of the roof. What induced the builders to site the cottage above the water-table I cannot imagine. The spring emerged just below my track, and was piped to a well fifty yards down the front field, where its overflow was piped on to provide the water supply for the farmhouse out of sight at the bottom of the hill. There were two rainwater-butts, fifty gallons in all, which would do for the garden or for washing, though the water needed to be boiled before it was fit for drinking, while the spring water was sweeter than any tap water.

There are not many places left like this. The cottage is part of a big estate, but when all the other estate buildings were modernized, it was decided that Penlan was just too remote to make it worthwhile, so it was left as it stood, with no electricity, no gas, no running water or plumbing. No one had lived here for nearly fifty years, it was a relic of a way of life long gone, which the world no longer wanted. It was the highest and remotest cottage on the estate, but was also considered to be the one with the most outstanding view. The mountains on the southern horizon were twenty-five miles away. Many other homes in the area gave a glimpse of these far hills, but most houses were built in little valleys or folds in the mountain, or somewhere there was a modicum of shelter from the elements. Penlan had been built without any consideration for the comfort of its occupants and was on such a high, exposed ridge that its horizon was a panoramic sweep that stretched fifty miles or more from east to west. It hovered over the world.

My friends had taken on the cottage earlier that year and had visited just once. They had attempted to start a fire, and the chimney had caught alight from the generations of jackdaw nests that filled it. After my first visit, I came again and again, I spent Christmas there, and saw in the New Year at the very top of my mountain. It takes longer to climb than you expect; there is one false summit after another, and then you suddenly reach the hilltop cairn almost as you are upon it. Sitting at the cairn you can see only a disc of around fifty yards around you, then the hillside falls away too steeply to be seen. It was a clear night and there was barely any grass there, just a forest of silvery lichen that looked almost fluorescent in the moonlight. The neighbouring peaks were smeared with snow, and all around there was a frozen silence.

On New Year's Day I had planned a serious walk, but it poured with rain, so I spent much of the day sitting in the porch looking out. On the mounded rocks of Penlan Farm a big ash bough had long since fallen, too long ago for it to be any use for the fire. A great spotted woodpecker flew in from the trees in crisp black and white. No red on its crown, so a female, but a beautiful cherry-red rump. She began to hack away at the rotten wood, sawdust flying every which way. Over the course of an hour, seemingly oblivious to the heavy rain, she hammered out a fair-sized hole, pausing only to gulp down grubs. Eventually a stoat stuck its nose out from under the trunk; I swear it looked disgruntled at having been woken by the constant drumming above its head. It peered out at the weather, then finally ventured out and ran over to the quieter shelter of a nearby hollow oak. Stoats are normally full of vitality, they bound and prance and undulate as they go, but this animal was positively slinking, its black-tipped tail dragging behind it.

That spring I took over the tenancy of the cottage, paying a peppercorn rent of just a hundred pounds a year. A house that is lived in falls apart much more slowly than one that is abandoned. My friends had decided it was not for them, even as a holiday let. They had been offered the use of another cottage on the estate with better facilities. There was a big house over the river where the lord and lady lived, but much of the estate had been shared out among their children, so my landlords were actually the eldest son and his wife, whom I had known for years. I moved in at the beginning of April, having burned what few bridges I had left. I unlocked the doors of the cottage and hung up the keys on a handy hook just inside. And I don't believe I have ever touched them since.

The first thing I needed to do was to make the place habitable, by my standards if not by those of others. I mended the gates and the fence to keep the sheep out of the little garden so it would be usable. A lot of roof tiles had slipped, so I fixed them back in place using the little strips of lead that undoubtedly have a name but which remains unknown to me. The ceiling of the main bedroom had collapsed, so I nailed up squares of plasterboard and roughly filled the gaps. I am no handyman; it looked a complete mess. But it worked, and still works now. The downpipe that led from the gutter to one of the water-butts had snapped off at the top. I filled the gap with a plastic funnel, a short length of hosepipe, and some gaffer tape. And that did the job for the next five years. The narrow gap behind the back wall of the house and the quarry wall was inclined to flood from the overflow from the water-butts and the rain that ran down the rock face, so I dug a trench and filled it with gravel and a length of cast-off land drain that I found in the corner of a field. Rain would run down the chimney into the fire, so I climbed the stack and cemented a couple of spare slate roof tiles over it in an upside-down V. I fashioned a cowling for the chimney-place out of a sheet of aluminium I found in the woodshed, to stop so much smoke backing into the room. And so the house was ready for me.

A hundred years ago, when the cottage was a family home, the place would have been better equipped for living. In the kitchen at the back of the house was an old copper for heating water, but it was rusted beyond repair now, and the fireplace beneath it had been bricked in, as had the bread ovens beside it. Even the chimney had been blocked off. I say kitchen, but perhaps scullery is a better description for a room with no water and no cooking facilities. But it was where I stored my jugs of water for the day's use, and my pots and pans, and there was a stone sink and a walk-in pantry that here at the north of the house never saw a ray of sun and so kept things reasonably cool throughout the year. There was another copper in the woodshed where once laundry would have been washed, but this too was no longer usable.

It was spring and there was life all around me as I worked. A pair of starlings nested in the corner of the gable, and all day long they perched at the very top of the ash immediately in front of the house and mimicked everything they heard, so I would keep rushing out to look for things that weren't there. They did a particularly fine curlew. The jackdaws had steered clear of the smoking chimney, and built their nest in a hollow in the ash at the back of the house. This ash tree grew straight out of the rock of my quarry wall; it never seemed to have enough leaves and looked as though it might come crashing down at any time. But it never did. Pied wagtails had tucked themselves away in the drystone wall that separated my garden from the track. This is a bird whose nest is notoriously hard to find; the feeding birds would land on a rock some distance away, their beaks stuffed with insects, their tails bobbing, then scurry along the track in the lee of the wall to throw predators off the scent. It took several days of watching closely to locate the exact spot, in a little niche in the rocks not a foot above the ground. The parent birds were never out of sight, they found enough food in the field within fifty yards of the nest. I felt protective of these birds; they were the welcoming committee to my new home, and in the Gypsy tradition they are a bird of good omen. Two of the chicks left the nest long before they were ready, when they were just nine days old, two tiny bundles of innocence huddled together on a nearby rock, cheeping for their parents. Lots of young birds leave the nest days before they can fly, and it seems like a risky survival strategy; they are just so vulnerable to predators. But I suppose that when the young are competing against one another for a limited supply of food, it is the birds that leave the nest first that get fed first. When I heard the alarm calls of the parent birds and saw them fluttering in distress, I went out and chased away the squirrel that had come too close and was sniffing around with interest, and took the two little feather-balls back to their nest. They stayed there all day but by nightfall they were out again. I was relieved to find them alive in the morning, and in fact the whole brood fledged successfully. It doesn't pay to get too attached to the fate of individual birds though; it's a brutal life out there in the fields and forests. Small birds like blue tits will lay a clutch of thirteen or fourteen eggs, and if things go well will try for a second clutch, which gives some idea of their life chances; if mortality was not so high they would be everywhere, swarming like locusts.

On an unexpectedly warm spring day I threw open the doors to air the place. A swallow flew in through the open front door, circled me three times where I stood in the centre of the living room, then exited through the back door as suddenly as it had arrived. For a moment inside became outside, my cottage became a part of the landscape, not a self-contained unit that separated me from the natural world beyond its windows.

In the loft was a small breeding colony of bats, and it was a pleasure on a mild evening to sit out in the garden at dusk and count them out. They would dart out from invisible crevices under the eaves and head straight for the trees; these were long-eared bats that specialize in picking insects off leaves, rather than concentrating on flying insects. There were sometimes one or two Natterer's bats too, slightly larger and rarer, that zoomed off into the distance. It is not easy to identify bat species, even in the hand, let alone as they dart around at frantic speed in the half-light. Only a decade ago experts finally realized that the pipistrelle, our most numerous and familiar bat, was actually two distinct species. Usually their manner of flight was my best clue that most of my residents were long-eareds, but sometimes I would catch the silhouette of ears that looked half the animal's body length and made them look like tiny flying rabbits. I stayed away from the loft in season; these colonies are so vulnerable that you need a licence to visit them. I generally counted about twenty or thirty bats emerging from my loft; come the summer the numbers would rise as the year's young began independent flight. Bats may look to us like winged mice, but their life cycles are very different: mice have just a year to breed a new generation, while bats can live for thirty years and occupy the same summer and winter roosts for the whole of their lives. That is why it is so important to protect their chosen sites; long-eareds in particular don't take kindly to new homes. They didn't leave the cottage only at dusk and return at dawn, but came and went all night, and when I stepped outside in the dark they would often be chasing each other in circles around and around the house. They would fly incredibly close, so that I could feel the breath of their wings on my skin, but they would never touch me, their reflexes were so fast. Sometimes at night I could hear the faint rustle of them moving around in the roof-space, and it felt like a privilege to know they were there, living out their unfathomable lives just above me.

Less welcome as house guests were the mice that invaded the house in the spring. Only once did I find I had house mice, which are something of a rarity in these parts. No, these were country mice rather than town mice, long-tailed field mice and their larger and less common cousins the yellow-necked mice that overflowed into the cottage from the fields. They were cute little critters with big black eyes, but they made a terrible mess and ate everything. There were five sturdy ham hooks embedded in the living-room ceiling, and I would hang vulnerable packages of food from these in carrier bags, but the mice had a remarkable propensity to find something, anything, that I had overlooked. They would gnaw their way happily through plastic containers and bottles, eat their way through corks, and were partial to a little nibble of soap. I didn't want to kill them so I got myself some live traps and released them back into the wild. They would make their way straight back from a surprising distance, so to be on the safe side I usually took them all the way to the far side of the river.

The daytimes I spent getting to know my patch. Though I took occasional forays further afield, to all intents and purposes my home turf was anywhere I could walk to and from in a day, and so it expanded in summer and contracted in winter. Loosely, it formed a rough circle with a perimeter five miles from the cottage. It was skewed though; I spent much less time on the east side of the river. This was not because of accessibility; although it was miles north or south to the nearest road bridges, at my nearest point on the river was a footbridge, a beautiful old suspension bridge that swayed and rolled as you walked across it, which was a fine place to pause and watch the dippers and grey wagtails for a while, and was a handy short cut to the main road beyond. But east of the river the hills grew steadily smaller and more populated as you headed in the direction of the Marches and England beyond, and I was drawn inexorably to the wild, and to the west.

The sheep-grazing fields immediately around the cottage, in spite of the vast views they afforded, felt secluded, flanked to the west by Penlan Wood, a fully grown plantation of Norway spruce, and to the east by a small oak wood long preserved as pheasant cover, misty with bluebells in the spring and above which loomed the rocky crags of the mountainside across the valley. The top field behind the house was capped by a long thicket of Scots pines, and a hundred yards downhill, as the hillside fell steeply away, was a scattering of massive oaks, many hundreds of years old and hollowed out with age. The top of Penlan Wood ran almost level with the cottage, and apart from that uninterrupted view directly west on to the moors the cottage was encircled by trees, as if in a large forest clearing. The only other person who came here was the farmer, to tend to his sheep, otherwise this was my own personal domain. Sometimes it felt as though I didn't need to go anywhere else, that if I just waited here patiently, every wild creature there was to be seen in mid-Wales would eventually come and visit me.

Penlan Wood was my shelter; it gave the cottage a modest amount of protection from the prevailing south-west wind. These conifer plantations have been vilified for despoiling natural habitats and being generally lifeless, and Penlan Wood seemed this way too. It was hard to get into, fringed with a tangle of rhododendrons that overhung its fence, and once you got inside it was dark and gloomy and still. No birds sang, and the ground was bare, just a thick mulch of pine needles. Nothing grew there, save in autumn when bright white eggs would emerge from the ground, from which would burst the other-worldly flyblown phalluses of stinkhorn toadstools. The wood had never been thinned, presumably because it was small, obscure, in an awkward location, and was easily forgotten. The trees were fully grown now, perhaps forty years old, and stood shoulder to shoulder so little light could penetrate the dense canopy. It was only a small plantation, just a few acres, and seemed totally unpromising, but it was there right beside me and it felt like mine. The place took time to give up its secrets, but this apparent lifelessness turned out to be an illusion.

Owls called each night from the edge of the wood. At its nearest corner was a single ancient oak. They say that oak trees take two hundred years to grow, two hundred years to live, and two hundred years to die. This tree was dying;

its topmost branches were leafless antlers. I wondered if this tree might be the owls' home, but when I inspected it there were no holes I could see that could possibly be used for nesting. And then one sunny day I was walking across the field past the tree, and the sun cast a perfect shadow replica of the oak on to the grass at my feet. I saw the shadow of an owl on the ground below me, and before I could even look up the ghost owl disappeared into the very heart of darkness. I watched the tree constantly after that, and in the evenings I would sit on a nearby tree stump and watch the owls' comings and goings. They didn't seem to mind; the female even paid me a return visit one afternoon. I was in the garden weeding when she flew over for a closer look, calling softly. The male and female were quite distinct, the male a pale grey bird, the female a dark rufous brown. When I knew for sure that both birds were out hunting, I shinned up the tree trunk to where the boughs spread, navigating my way around a clump of bramble that was growing from the fork. It was important to be sure they were both away; one early bird photographer lost an eye to a tawny owl, right here on this estate. They will attack anything they see as a predator after their chicks. The tree was completely hollow, the hole was a vertical chimney almost all the way down to ground level, over six feet deep. I didn't have a torch so I lowered down a storm lamp on the end of a length of string. And there at the bottom was a single comical-looking chick, with oversized feathered feet and the long tail of a half-eaten mouse emerging from its beak, which peered up at me and hissed at the light. Tawny owls' main prey is the field vole, but vole numbers fluctuate wildly from one year to the next. The size of the owls' clutch will depend on the availability of prey, and this was evidently not a good year for voles, as this solitary chick was far smaller than it should have been this late in the season.

In the heart of the wood nested woodpigeons, and a pair of magpies, while the carrion crows always chose an old oak in the fields near by. Along its bottom edge nested the buzzards, looking down over the oak and alder woods around the stream at the bottom of the hill. It was always the same pair; buzzards' markings vary hugely and it would have been possible to get to know every one of the local buzzards individually were there not so many of them. Often there would be twelve or fifteen of them circling over the hillside, squabbling over their territorial rights. For two or three years I would regularly see a buzzard that was all white apart from some brown on its wing feathers, it would often be out in my front field in the early morning, hunting for the night's worms. The Penlan Wood pair had been here for years, and there was a whole row of old nests along the flank of the wood. When the young lost their infant down and fledged they would loiter around the trees in the bottom field for a couple of weeks, mewling piteously for food. And then one year my home pair of buzzards elected to move nest, to the thick horizontal bough, strewn with polypody ferns, of a streamside oak, with the nest directly above the rushing mountain stream. It was a pretty spot, and much more conducive to watching the young as they grew.

Penlan Wood was not quite square. It had a fifth corner

facing west, almost directly south of the cottage just fifty yards downhill, and right on this corner was a small fox earth. There was another earth too in the pine wood above the cottage, and the two were evidently connected as I frequently saw foxes commuting between them. A direct route between them would have taken the foxes right past the cottage, but their path always followed a loop that kept them a safe distance away. These were shy animals; country foxes are much harder to watch than city foxes, and with good reason. The hunt began in earnest every autumn. These were farmers' hunts, not horseback hunts. They would bring the pack up the lanes in their Land Rovers, and follow them on foot with walkie-talkies. They never seemed to make it to my charmed clearing in the woods, but I would sometimes run into them while I was out walking, and they would eye me with suspicion, and after they were gone I would find the blooded corpses hung from trees. Seventy per cent of the year's young would be killed each year; if a fox made it through its first year it was probably too wily to be caught.

One day as I was walking past the wood and took a peek over the fence at the fox earth I noticed a broken shell right by the earth, and this was how I discovered that jays were nesting in a tree directly above the foxes' heads. Jays are beautiful birds, with their lilac breasts, barred hackles, and that incredible jolt of electric blue on their wings. They are conspicuous birds that clatter through the woods in family troupes, screeching raucously, and seem weak on the wing, loping from tree to tree as though they can barely keep themselves aloft. But in the nesting season they change completely, becoming secretive and silent and seemingly disappearing from view. I was able to watch closely as the nest site was in full view of my window. They would slip silently out of the wood almost at ground level, and dart straight for the cover of the nearest tree, like a different bird altogether.

One year rooks moved into Penlan Wood. The nearest rookery was a mile away at least, in a beech wood the other side of the river and up-valley. These rookeries are occupied for generation after generation. Some sites are hundreds of years old, so I don't know what induced these birds to form a breakaway colony this particular year. There were six pairs nesting close together in the nearest corner of the wood. The young all left their nests before they were fully fledged, and sat in the fields close to the fence all around the wood, their heads hunched into their shoulders. It was a bonanza for the foxes; every one was doomed. I watched a fox prancing across the front field on its way to its young in the pine wood above, the young rook still flapping in its jaws, the parent birds calling in protest and diving repeatedly at the fox, but not too close. The rooks never returned.

And then there were the sparrowhawks. I saw a sparrowhawk on my very first visit, down on the lanes skimming fast alongside a hedgerow, then suddenly flipping over the hedge to surprise unwary birds feeding in the field beyond. A couple of seconds and it was gone. Here one moment, gone the next; that is the way of the sparrowhawk. There is a ferocity in their burning eyes, and they live life at a different pace to the rest of the world; they never seem to rest, not for a moment. There can be no doubt that here is a creature whose heart beats twice as fast as ours. They seemed to me to epitomize the wildness I had come to seek, and I wanted to get to know them. It would not be easy, for they have good reason to be wary. They are the least favourite bird of the gamekeeper, and an old estate rule here was that nothing could be shot on a Sunday that wasn't for the pot, save for the sparrowhawk. I started to create a mental map of where and when I saw them, but there was no method to it; I might see them several times in a day, and then not for a week, and they could turn up anywhere at any time. My mental map was without trends, without clusters. But once I shifted my focus away from places and numbers and towards what they were doing when I saw them, it all started to make sense. I began to unlock their secrets, and eventually I would get to know every nesting site in the area. And the nearest of these was in Penlan Wood.

It was early spring and a female hawk was circling the wood. It is easy to tell the males and females apart: like many birds of prey the female is almost twice the size of the male, not in length but in bulk. The male bird is much more lightly built and falcon-like, with red barring on his pale breast and a slate-grey back, while the female is a dark grey-brown with broad short wings and a heftier build all round. There is good sense to this size difference as they don't compete for prey. The little males tend to concentrate on small birds like finches, while the female will take on bigger challenges such as pigeons. I first saw the female from my window beating her way up the hillside close to the edge of the wood, in a flight that was utterly distinctive and quite unlike the hawk's normal dash. Her wingbeats were slow and measured and she was just four or five feet above the ground; she looked like she had all the time in the world. Her tail was fanned almost like that of a hovering kestrel, and as she flew she rose and fell, undulating like a woodpecker. When she reached the corner of the wood she turned sharply and proceeded along its top edge, and a few minutes later, in a shaft of sunlight, she reappeared from around the bottom again, preceded by a little flock of panicking redwings. This carried on for hours, it was as if she was wrapping the wood up in a parcel. This is not a behaviour I have ever heard of before, but she did it every year without fail, and it was one of the many things I looked forward to seeing each spring. She was totally consistent, and this in a bird that I first took to be unpredictable. She always, always, circled the wood anticlockwise.

When she finally tired of beating her way round and round the wood, the birds would engage in their much more familiar spring display flight. This is highly characteristic and your best chance of watching the bird for any protracted period. They rise high above their nesting wood and fly in tight circles above the site, for once making themselves deliberately conspicuous and visible from far off, presumably to indicate their whereabouts to the birds in neighbouring territories and stake their claim. Every now and again they will suddenly plummet down into the wood, often to the exact tree where they will build their nest. And this is how I first found their nesting site, close to the north-west corner of Penlan Wood, facing out on to the moors. There were three old nests in adjacent trees, for like the buzzards they prefer not to reuse old nests but choose to build a new one next door. Having found the site I kept clear, for I didn't want to disturb them.

The jays raised four young in their nest above the fox earth. As soon as the fledglings were on the wing, they moved down to the broadleaved woods by the stream, and reverted to their customary ways, crashing in a noisy troupe from tree to tree, announcing their presence with raucous cries. They would have done better to stay silent, for each time I saw the family there seemed to be one less, picked off by the sparrowhawks. Over the course of two weeks, I found the remains of three of them, a flash of blue among the leaf litter, a scatter of lilac down.

A sunny morning in late spring, and I was sitting on my doorstep looking out over a silent hillside. The sparrow-hawk pair burst from behind the cottage, one to the left and one to the right. They were flying straight out at great speed, the ground falling away beneath them. As they reached the bottom of the front field, the little male plunged down, then turned and swooped directly up at his mate, as if he were about to attack her from beneath. As he reached her he rolled on to his back and locked talons with her, and the two birds started to tumble downwards, wings flailing wildly. Just as it seemed they were beyond the point of no return and would be dashed on the ground, they sep-arated and raced into the woods below, their wingtips brushing the tops of the long grass. It was a breathtaking display of aerial mastery that was over in seconds but was unforgettable. As quickly as they appeared they were gone, leaving just the fields basking in the morning sunshine, and the hillside ringing with a sudden emptiness.

2. *A Gathering Silence*

The farmer had been out in the front field all day long, grubbing up thistles. He was fighting a constant battle with the thistles that invaded his fields; a battle he was losing, at least in this field, which was rapidly becoming overgrown not just with thistles but with bracken, nettles and sedges too. Personally I liked the thistles, they brought in the tinkling flocks of goldfinches that would winkle out the seeds with their sharp beaks; but then I wasn't trying to scratch a living out of this land. I invited the farmer in for a cup of tea and he came to join me. He was a heavily built man, amiable and slow-moving, a man of few words, which suited me just fine, but on this occasion he opened up a little. He worked in partnership with his brother, who lived in the neighbouring farmhouse with his family. That farm had been bought, while this one was still tenanted. He told me he regretted never having had a family of his own, but he had stayed at home until he was in his forties to tend to his ailing parents, and by then it was too late to find a wife. The sheep on both the brothers' farms were dyed in the wool, not with their initials, but their father's.

He said he could remember from his childhood when Penlan Cottage was still occupied full-time. He told me that the lady who lived here had died in the cottage, and had to be taken to chapel for burial. Not to the village

church, but to a chapel miles further away. She was a big
lady, he said, a very big lady, and the most direct route to
chapel was over the tops. The coffin was carried down to
the bridge near where my postbox was now, and up the
hillside beyond. The incline here is extremely steep, it
would have been an arduous climb even unburdened. He
said he watched for hours as the pall-bearers inched their
way up the mountain under their heavy load. It took them
twelve hours in total to get to chapel.

Although it was over forty years since anyone had lived
here year-round, the cottage had been used in summer, so
there was a modicum of furnishings: beds, a table, a couple
of wardrobes, some old tools in the woodshed. When I
moved in I took nothing with me but a bag of clothes. This
was a conscious choice; I had decided I would start with
nothing, and work my way up to a bare minimum. I wanted
to know how lightly I could tread on the earth.

My friends who had first let the cottage, and then
decided it was not for them, offered to sell me their two-
ring cooker. But I thought: why commit myself to hauling
gas bottles up the mountainside when there was a perfectly
serviceable fire? The fireplace was actually equipped for
cooking, with a solid metal bar across the centre and a
selection of S-hooks of varying lengths to hang your pots
from. There was already a big old hanging kettle here,
black with soot, which would be in constant use. I picked
up a beautiful cast-iron skillet from an abandoned farmhouse, a friend gave me a witch's cauldron that she found
for me in a car-boot sale, and later another gave me a Dutch
oven, with a lid so heavy it was virtually a pressure cooker.

It is easy to become complacent about eating when you live alone, but I made sure I cooked proper meals each day. If I had to soak beans overnight, then spend two hours cooking up a cauldron of stew, then so be it; I had the time. I became proficient at cooking over the fire, and it seemed more natural than cooking on a hob. When my biggest-ever group of guests arrived unexpectedly, it was no problem to rustle up a meal for ten. Visitors would sometimes try to replicate my meals when they got home, but said they never tasted as good. I don't know if it was the slight smokiness that infused everything, the thickness of the pans, or just the setting, but it was true: food tasted better here.

At a turn in the river there is a wide bank of pale grey shingle filled with flood pools, where the mallards dabble, and overgrown with a wood of mature alders. The wood regularly floods, but the alders don't mind the occasional dunking. Every time there was a spate the trees would end up festooned with flotsam: branches, leaves, fertilizer bags, even car tyres. It is an other-worldly place. I was exploring this stretch of the river a few months after first moving to the cottage when I had a curious find. As I walked through the trees I saw a face coming towards me. It was my own face, in the intact wing mirror of a car that had lodged in the crook of an alder at head height, and I speculated on the history that had led it to this place. I had not seen myself in weeks, there were no mirrors in the house, but now I had a shaving mirror.

At first I had no way of telling the time either, I just lived by the rhythms of the sun, but then I was given a little transistor radio. It was nice to be able to listen to music occasionally if I wanted to, though mostly I chose silence. And it was useful to be able to find out the time, if for example I wanted to cross the river to the main road and catch the postbus to town, which came only once a day. Though usually I preferred to hitch, because then I could simply stroll down to the road at whatever time suited me.

The decision not to have a vehicle was critical. It changed the scale of things entirely. To me, the pocket of wild country I lived in felt remote, but the nearest town, a very small town admittedly, was only seven miles away. That's a long walk, but only a short hop in a car. These are small islands. I knew that if I walked to the main road in the morning and started hitching, I could be in a nightclub in London that night. And because I knew that I could, I didn't have to. Hitching coast to coast in America took me nearly two weeks, and in Australia my longest lift was over a thousand miles, because that's how far it was to the next city. That's a distance equivalent to travelling from Britain to Africa. And I had to wait thirty-six hours by the road-side to get that lift. Yet though I was living in a crowded country, the isolation at Penlan was real. Over five years I kept count of the number of passers-by who came walking up my track. Not one. The track simply didn't go any-where; it followed a circuitous route from the middle of nowhere to the back of beyond. People who wanted to hillwalk generally went to the Brecon Beacons further south, or Snowdonia to the north. These hills and moors midway between them, with slightly lower peaks, were for the most part left to me and the birds.

In summer it was usually possible to get a car up to the cottage, though you had to open and close seven gates on your way up the track, and the final steep slope defeated some people. In the wet, or when the leaves were falling, it was more touch-and-go, and in the winter it was pretty much four-wheel drive only. Summer was a sociable time for me, by my standards. I am by no means an antisocial person, in fact I had hitherto lived a life in which I chose to surround myself with people, and I now wanted to know who I was when I could no longer define myself in terms of my relation to others. When I first moved to the cottage, I had no idea whether I would be able to cope with living alone, whether I could live with myself. Friends would come for weekend visits, or sometimes longer. It was like a camping holiday for them, with my cottage a stone tent. They would come bearing gifts, boots filled with canned goods and crates of beer. Sometimes they would bring musical instruments, and we would have a jam session around the fire. I would enjoy showing them my haunts and introducing them to the local wildlife, and I would keep them busy hauling wood up the hillside. It was nearly always up; there was very little dead wood above me, I was so close to the treeline. No wood, no fire, I would say. No fire, no dinner. The real hard work was not sawing the logs or splitting them, it was getting the wood to the cottage in the first place. And when after a few days my guests departed, I would wave them off and think: Well, that was nice, but now back to real life. And I would feel a palpable, if slightly guilty, twinge of relief. And perhaps they would feel a sense of relief too, at heading back to the comforts of home.

Sawing logs for the fire with a handsaw was incredibly time-consuming, so I picked up an old chainsaw that had seen better days, which made my life a whole lot easier. The farmer would sometimes tell me of a tree which had blown down across one of his fences, and say that if I logged it he would bring it up to me with his tractor, which was a godsend. The chainsaw also had the added advantage of allowing me to earn a little money. It wasn't good enough for clear-felling, but there were smaller jobs in these outlying woods, like thinning out twenty-year-olds, that weren't worth sending in a team for. With no rent to speak of, and no bills, I didn't need to earn much. I would write the occasional article and send it off for publication, and down near the village was the field centre for the University of Wales. The doctor who ran the place was a mine of information on local natural history, everybody came to him with their observations, and he would occasionally ask me to help out with a research project. All of these pieces of work had two things in common: I could do as little or as much as I wanted, whenever I wanted, and I could do them almost entirely alone, hardly ever having to see another person. In spring I got busy with two projects that I undertook every year. I had a hundred and twenty bird boxes in the woods that I checked weekly, recording the laying dates, the dates the birds began to brood, when they hatched. And finally, when the young birds were ready, I would ring the fledglings. And I had a four-mile beat of the river that I monitored for the river-bird survey. These two projects occupied me two days a week for several months each year.

I don't recall ever having felt bored, not for a moment, in the same way that I don't recall a moment of loneliness. There was simply too much to do, and this was a life lived without any of the time-saving devices that we take for granted. There was always firewood waiting to be chopped, and water that needed to be hauled. Just making a cup of tea would take ten times as long as elsewhere; there was no switch to flick. If there was no rain for two weeks, the water-butts would run dry, and all my water had to come from the well. With the reputation that Wales has for rain, this may seem unlikely, but in fact it would happen twice every year, once in summer and once in winter. On just a couple of occasions the well ran dry too, and I had to carry water all the way up the hill from the stream. The longest drought I ever experienced was six weeks; much more frequently there would be daily rain for weeks. The weather here is unpredictable, and it can change from one minute to the next. I remember one clear, sunny day in early summer I was coming down off the hill when I was overtaken by a sudden hailstorm. The hailstones were the largest I had ever seen, the size of marrowfat peas, and it had been so mild I was not even wearing a jacket. I pulled my jumper over my head and ran for home, the stones bouncing off my knuckles. There is no use railing against the weather, it is out of our hands. All you can do is learn to live with it, and welcome it in all its variety.

I had a daily routine dictated by the simplicity of my lifestyle, and an annual routine too, led by the seasons, the elements. We insulate ourselves against the world outside our windows, so that our lives can carry on regardless. Peel away those layers of insulation and the cycles of the natural world regain their true importance. I even developed my own rituals, such as seeing in the New Year from the summit of my hill. At the summer solstice, I would not sleep; I would walk overnight through the darkness deep into the hills, to see the sun rise on the longest day from a mountain top. Long before the first rays of light came over the horizon, as soon as there was the barest lifting of the darkness, the snipe would begin their strange drumming display flights, falling from the sky with the wind bleating through their tail feathers.

I couldn't feel lonely. Loneliness is the product of an isolation that has not been freely chosen. You can of course feel more lonely in the midst of a crowd of people if those people are not giving you the human contact you desire, in the same way that poverty surrounded by affluence feels harsher, more shocking, than poverty shared. Solitude embraced is the opposite of loneliness. Friends would occasionally ask why I didn't get myself a dog, for company, but of course they were missing the point: that I was trying to understand the meaning of a life lived without company. Having a pet would have felt like a compromise. And on a practical level, this was a far less suitable place for a dog than it appeared at first sight. I took care of a friend's dog once for a week or so while the owner was on holiday. The dog was a Welsh border collie just like the farmer's sheepdogs, but she had been born in the city and lived there all her life, and had never seen a sheep before. She spent her entire time hunkered down in the long grass in the garden, her eyes fixed on the sheep in the field below. And when I took her out for walks, I could never let her off the lead, for nowhere could be guaranteed sheep-free. It must have been a week of intense frustration for her.

In the summertime I generally bathed in the river. Often I would make a day of it, taking a packed lunch and striking out over the hill to a favourite location: a wide beach of smooth disks of slate, perfect for skimming, and a deep pool. The water off the mountains was always cold, but if the sun was warm it didn't matter. I would spend hours there: bathing, swimming, washing my hair and my clothes. In the winter I would boil up kettlefuls of water and have strip-washes in front of the fire. Or there was a holiday let down by the river where they would leave the key in the porch for me so I could go in and use their bath and washing machine. A cheat perhaps, if this had been a dare, but there were no rules other than those I decided for myself as I went along.

Every week or two I would walk to the village shop to buy staples: tea, coffee, sugar, and so on. There was a petrol station in the village too, where I could get petrol for my chainsaw, and a couple of pubs, though I never felt tempted to walk down to the village of an evening for a night out. Not once. Rather than following the lanes, I would take a more direct and scenic route – through fields, over fences, along the riverbank. I could get there in just over an hour if I didn't dawdle, though I usually did. Down the track past my little oak wood, then across a field towards the beech hanger. There was a tongue of bracken-covered moorland alongside the wood here, and the hillside fell sharply beneath the overhanging beech boughs. At the bottom of the wood there was a footpath that ran south the whole length of the wood. There were views of the river below, and it was a fine, full-grown beech wood, a haze of blue in the spring. The path eventually led to a bridge where my stream met the river. This was the head of the lanes; the track up to the farm and Penlan began here. There was a turning circle, which was also the point for rubbish collection, so I would drop mine off; I usually generated about a carrier bag's worth a month. I would cross a footbridge over the long-abandoned railway track and follow the riverbank. About halfway to the village there was a break in the trees that fringed the riverside. A nice grassy spot to pause for a while, with a fallen tree to sit on, and a big shingly island where the common sandpipers nested. Another stream joined the river here; in summer I would pick my way across it on wobbly stepping stones, while in winter I would take a running jump and hope to clear it.

The bank became virtually impassable beyond this point, so I would cross a field on to the route once taken by the railway. I started in a deep cutting, overarched by trees, dark and boggy and filled with nettles. There was the ancient, rusted wreck of a car here that must have been rolled down the bank well over fifty years ago; I couldn't tell the make but it had running boards. It felt as though I was walking through a tunnel. There was a tangible sense of history here, but soon the trees gave way and the sun came in. Here in the cutting walls I once saw a pair of weasels popping their heads in and out of a niche in the rocks. I always looked out for them every time I passed this way, but I never saw them here again. The ground fell away and I was on a bridge, not a tunnel, with the fields twenty feet below me to either side. But the real bridge over the river was long gone. The river here turned sharply, and tumbling over rocks it had gouged out a sheer bank perhaps forty feet high. I crossed one last stream, on a bridge of two logs, and the last part of my journey was through dense woodland high over the river. First mixed woodland, then stands of old conifers where the sparrow-hawks nested. I would watch out for them here, and sometimes I would even see them over the village. Finally I would emerge from the woods and, after crossing one field of head-high corn, come to the road-bridge that led to the village.

Just past the bridge was a fine beach with a swimming hole, and I would often pause here for a while if the weather was good. In spite of its proximity to the village there was almost never anyone else here. As I stepped into the water thousands of tiny fish would dart away from the shallows, and before long there would be a loud *chikeee* and a lightning bolt in neon blue would flash past. The kingfishers nested in the bank here every year without fail, even though the village boys would sometimes stopper their holes with stones as a game. It was a good place to bring guests; even people with no real interest in birds like to see a kingfisher – they are just so glamorous and unexpectedly tiny, and the sighting was almost guaranteed.

After loading up with supplies, I would need to make a decision; whether to retrace my steps along the riverbank or walk back along the lanes. Almost anyone who lived along these lanes and who passed by would stop and give me a lift, but there were not many of them, and I could easily find myself walking the whole way back without a car passing. And it was a lot further. About a quarter of the way home from the village was my local telephone box, but I wouldn't stop. This would be a separate trip, on a Sunday when people would not be at work, but of course then the shop would not be open either.

I remember once walking to the village shop, collecting up my few basic requirements and taking them up to the counter, and as I spoke to the shopkeeper my voice cracked. It was only then that I realized I hadn't spoken a word in at least two weeks. It also made me aware that I never talked to myself, never sang to myself, not ever.

Going down to cross the river one day after I had already been at the cottage a year or two, I came upon a team of men renovating the old footbridge. It was probably not before time; I was used to it, but my visitors would sometimes be alarmed by how it swayed and rocked. If you walked fast, it would roll like a wave under your feet, and the suspension would creak and groan. And it was a long way down to the rocky waters below. I got chatting to the foreman of the gang, and found that his family was the last to live at Penlan. He had lived there until he was seven, when the family had decanted to town. He asked me if I snared many rabbits up there, and I said none at all, as I was vegetarian. Then he asked the route I followed into the village, and was delighted to discover that my chosen path was almost identical to his daily walk to the village school. The railway bridge was still standing then, which would have cut out that final dog-leg, and reduced the journey time a little, but even so it was an astonishing distance for a five-year-old to cover twice a day. And he had to be there at seven o'clock sharp, or face the consequences. I asked him if he could conceive of living that life now, and he said absolutely, he loved it, except . . . except for one thing. He could not imagine life without a television.

Less often I travelled into town, which had a health-food shop where I could stock up on dried pulses for my one-pot stews and fine-ground flour for the unleavened bread I made on a griddle over the fire. There was a hardware store for paraffin for my lamps and seeds for the garden, and a library. Occasionally I would take the daily postbus, but usually I hitchhiked. These were not busy roads, but I got lifts from regulars. The Travellers from a nearby site would stop for me without fail, as did a retired man who lived up-valley opposite the quarry. He would always tell me when the peregrines had returned to their eyrie. He'd spent his entire working life researching foxes for the Ministry of Agriculture, and was now spending his entire retirement travelling to and from the nearest golf course. In view of his wealth of experience, I asked him his opinion on whether or not foxes are pests. After some consideration he said: No, foxes are not pests, the foxes were here first. People are pests.

It was not a large garden. I say garden, but perhaps I should say the area around the cottage enclosed by a fence, for it had few attributes to distinguish it from the fields across that fence, although in February there would be a drift of snowdrops under my fruit tree, soon to be followed first by crocuses and then by huge numbers of daffodils. Long ago, someone had planted a scattering of bulbs, and over the years they had divided and divided so that each bulb became a cluster, and now in March the cottage would be surrounded by hundreds of nodding golden heads. Without the sheep coming in to trim it, the grass grew in rank tussocks that I had to hack back with a sickle. Besides the fruit tree, the jackdaw ash and the cotoneaster next to the porch, there was one small rhododendron and a clump of blackthorn by the gate. Once, before my time, a solitary pine had stood guard over the house from above the quarry wall, but it had been unlucky. The landlords, fearing that the ash balanced on the rocks would come crashing down on the cottage roof, had sent up a man to fell it, and he had mistakenly taken out the pine instead. The ash lived on to teeter another day, and teeters still, twenty years later. All that remains of the pine is its stump, a favoured perch for the green woodpeckers when they visit. I planted out a larch to stand in for the lonesome pine, and in the southwest corner of the garden a beech, which will one day afford the cottage a little shelter from the prevailing wind. Then a couple of rowans, for berries for the birds, and a buddleia for the butterflies. Apart from a row of poppies and wild flowers along the fence, I didn't trouble with flowers. I needed the land for food.

Although I planted a patch of herbs – coriander, dill and parsley, which were unavailable locally – my priority was the heavy vegetables. I didn't want to be hauling sackfuls of potatoes up the mountainside when I could be growing them myself. Preparing the land was hard work; the roots of the grass grew deep and tangled. Then I had to pick out all the rocks, carefully lift any daffodil bulbs for transplantation elsewhere, and lime the soil. Each year I would dig an extra patch, and prepare another for the next year by pegging down a sheet of tarpaulin with bricks to kill off the grass. I didn't want to use any pesticides, and besides the lime I bought no fertilizer. Each winter, when the bats were long gone to their hibernation roost, I would clamber up into the loft and shovel up bagfuls of guano. It was dry and powdery and odourless, and it seemed somehow appropriate that the bats who shared my home with me should help me grow my food.

I had never grown anything before, I had never stayed in one place long enough to even think about it, and had no idea what would grow well at this altitude, and in a location so exposed to the elements, so it was a process of trial and error. Each year I would try a few new things; if they grew well they would become a fixture; if they failed I would abandon them and try something else. I had a small patch of early potatoes, and a larger patch of main crops. I got a metal dustbin which I kept in the pantry and would fill it to the top with these, enough to last the whole year. Onions and garlic I hung on strings on the woodshed wall, as the mice didn't ever bother them. Garlic was the only thing I planted in autumn; growing garlic seems magical in its simplicity. Take a head of garlic, break it into cloves and plant them in a row. By the next year each clove will have turned into a new head.

Carrots and parsnips I stored in the ground and lifted when I needed them. The carrots in particular were a revelation; they are hard to grow in most places because of the depredations of the carrot fly, but the altitude here kept my crop pest-free. They grew to over a pound in weight without becoming woody, were such a deep orange they were almost red, and tasted better than any others I have had before or since. My first year I grew a fine crop of broad beans, but the next year and the one after they were infested by blackfly just as the pods were beginning to swell. The blackfly brought a fungal infection that wiped out the entire crop, so reluctantly I had to give up on them. My biggest problem was finding the right green vegetable. I could pick wild greens in season – sorrel and nettle tops, occasionally watercress from the mountain streams – but I needed something that I could rely on. Cabbages were destroyed by flea beetles, and though I managed a small crop of kale it was riddled with holes. Spinach was too inclined to bolt and had a short season. Then I found spinach beet, untroubled by pests and hardy enough to survive the worst of the winter's frosts. I could dust away the snow and pluck the fresh leaves below, so I had a supply of greens year-round. But if there is a satisfaction to be had from selecting and picking food you have grown yourself as and when it is time to eat, I found far more pleasure in foraging for wild food. Perhaps I am more in touch with my inner hunter-gatherer than my inner pastoralist.

The mushroom season began in late summer. These Welsh hills are renowned for their hallucinogenic psilocybin mushrooms. In a good year they would be hidden under every tussock of grass, their potency belied by how drab and inconspicuous they were. But I am talking here about edible mushrooms. Not so much the familiar field mushroom, which I seldom came across, though I would often find horse mushrooms in the fields, bigger and firmer and with a whiff of aniseed. A ring of them would always appear under the old ash just across the fence from my fruit tree, so I didn't have far to go for them. One year though, there was an incredible glut of field mushrooms, the year the farmer decided to plough and reseed the top field. This field had last been ploughed over twenty years ago, and I would be told the full story by the farmer.

In my front field just over the track lay an old harrow. It had been there so long it had sunk into the ground with only a few tines emerging through the grass to catch out the unwary. This is the way here; there seemed to be rusting pieces of farming equipment in the corner of every field, apparently forgotten but actually not, just waiting until they were next required. Even if that wait was twenty years or more. The farmer came up the track with his tractor and a chain and dragged the harrow out of the ground, then called me out to see the voles' nest he had unearthed. The nest was a soft ball of finely cut grass, and the baby voles were pink and blind and hairless. I held the nest in my hands, then we replaced it carefully under a sod of turf.

The hillside here was steep, extremely steep in places, and when it had last been ploughed the tractor had tipped right over and trapped the farmer beneath it. He lay pinned there all day, until he was missed at dinner time and his relatives came looking for him. His pelvis had been crushed and he never walked freely again. Once the top field had been ploughed and harrowed again, without incident this

time, and before the new seed had started to sprout, while
the field was still seemingly lifeless, bare brown earth, the
mushrooms appeared during the night. Great drifts of
white, as if there had been a snowfall. In a single trip I collected ten to fifteen pounds of them without making much
visible difference. The smaller ones, their gills still pale
pink, I reserved for cooking; the bigger ones with black-
ened gills I chopped up and salted down in buckets. In a
few days this produced over two litres of mushroom
ketchup, seasoning that would last me for years.

There is not much of a tradition in Britain of collecting
forest mushrooms, people seem wary of them, but I had
lived in Sweden, where foraging in the woods in autumn is
practically a national pastime, so I knew my mushrooms.
The first to come into season, in August or even sometimes
July, were the chanterelles. They grew in the dingle by my
stream, though only on the north bank. I never found a
single one on the southern bank, where instead there were
forest orchids, narrow-leaved helleborines, which never
crossed the stream either. Chanterelles are beautiful mushrooms, glowing apricot in colour, and many of mine were
a variety tinged with a dusting of amethyst. It was like
finding precious jewels shining in the leaf litter, in the
darkness under the thick trees. And they are a great mushroom to pick, both for flavour and for the fact that they are
completely untroubled by the mushroom flies, whose
worms ruin many species of mushroom before they are big
enough to eat. There would be more than I could eat so I
would preserve them to extend their short season. It is easy
enough to dry mushrooms, but they lose so much of their

flavour in the process. Instead, I would cook them in their own juices and a little vinegar, then drain and pack them in jars with dill and coriander seeds from the garden, then fill the jars to the brim with olive oil, taking care to shake out any trapped bubbles of air. And that way they would last me until their season began again.

As the chanterelles came to an end, the mushroom season proper began. Most visible of all were the parasols. Tall and elegant in white and fawn, they seemed to fringe every field and every track. When fully grown their caps can be as big as a plate, and I would coat them in batter or breadcrumbs and fritter them whole. There were far more of them than could possibly be eaten. There must have been at least fifteen types of mushroom that I collected and ate regularly; to my tastes, the best of all was the cep, with a thick, bulging stalk and a rich chestnut cap with yellow gills. They also grew down at the dingle by the stream, but only in small numbers and they never seemed to appear in the same place twice, so finding one was always a pleasant surprise. I would break the cap in two to check for worms; if they were unaffected, one mushroom would be enough for a meal.

And then there were the berries. I would make thirty jars of jam each year – not that I needed thirty jars for myself, but they made an appropriate gift for departing guests. There were brambles everywhere, especially along the lanes and the abandoned cart track by my stream, and blackberry jam would account for perhaps ten jars' worth. Blackberrying had been a feature of my childhood; there is a sense of innocence to it, the prickles snagging on your clothes, the purple-stained fingers. There were a few wild strawberries along the lanes, but these were too small to be anything more than a treat in passing. On the steep hillside beyond my postbox was a mature plantation, five or ten times the size of my own little Penlan Wood, and in the very heart of it was a hidden clearing that I had stumbled upon. It was filled with wild raspberries. A few jars of raspberry jam, and plenty more for eating fresh. Halfway down the track to the farm were the remains of another farmhouse or labourer's cottage. The barest trace of it remained, less even than of Penlan Farm, but there were two damson trees beside the ruins. It was ironic that the fruit trees they had planted had long outlived their home. I had to compete with the blackbirds and thrushes, but would always get enough for a few jars of plum jam to add to the store.

Bilberry jam was the biggest treat, to be stirred into steaming hot porridge on a winter's morning. Bilberries thrive where the heather grows deep and tall, and most of the hills here were far too heavily grazed for heather. If I found bilberry plants at all on my hill, they would be stunted and cropped to an inch high, and would seldom fruit at all. But there was one hillside that had been protected from heavy grazing, where the heather blazed purple as summer ended, and I would head here every year for a basket of berries. It was a longish walk upriver, through a tiny village with no shops at all where the swifts screamed all summer long. The hillside, waist-high in heather, was fringed by beautiful hanging oak woods and had a character all its own; more like a dry heath than the wet, boggy moorland I was used to. Cuckoos called constantly here in season, and I once found the egg case of a grass snake, the only sign I ever saw of one. The land here was too cold and damp for reptiles; I would occasionally see a common lizard or a slow-worm sunning itself on a rock, but even these were a novelty.

If there was a shortfall on my target figure of thirty jars, I would make up the difference with crab jelly. My top field had a scattering of crab apples on it; they didn't fruit every year but seemed to take turns, so that every year one single tree would be laden with hard little apples. The jelly was quite plain so I would flavour the jars variously; with sloes from the blackthorns by my gate, with elderberries from the hedgerows, or with rowanberries from the mountain ashes in the hills.

I experimented with making alcohol, using an old recipe I had found for elderflower champagne. It bubbled away for a month on the stone shelf in my pantry until it was time for bottling. I took a sip; it was foul, so in my disappointment I just shoved the bottles to the back of my shelves and forgot about them. A year later, I needed the bottles, so I took them out to tip the experiment away. Almost as an afterthought I decided to give it another try, and it was absolutely delicious. Some sort of alchemy had taken place over the year they had been left undisturbed. So that too became a part of my annual routine; elders were everywhere so I could make as much as I wanted.

By the time the first frosts came in November, my shelves would be laden with jars of jam and pickled mushrooms, bottles of ketchup and wine, and whatever else I had preserved that year. What vegetables could not be left out to overwinter would be harvested and stored. I would be like a squirrel with my cache of nuts to keep me through the hard times to come. The hatches would be battened down; I was ready for the worst. Happiness is a full larder.

This was the pattern of my days, a simple life led by natural rhythms rather than the requirements and expectations of others. Imagine being given the opportunity to take time out of your life, for five whole years. Free of social obligations, free of work commitments. Think how well you would get to know yourself, all that time to consider your past and the choices you had made, to focus on your personal development, to know yourself through and through, to work out your goals in life, your true ambitions.

None of this happened, not to me. Perhaps for someone else it would have been different. Any insight I have gained has been the result of later reflection. Solitude did not breed introspection, quite the reverse. My days were spent outside, immersed in nature, watching. I saw as much as I did because of two things: the first, quite simply, was time, the long hours spent out in the field; the second was alertness, a state of heightened attentiveness. My attention was constantly focused away from myself and on to the natural world around me. And my nights were spent sitting in front of the log fire, aimlessly turning a log from time to time and staring at the flickering flames. I would not be thinking of the day just gone; the day was done. And I would not be planning tomorrow; tomorrow would take care of itself. The silence outside was reflected by a growing silence within. Any interior monologue quietened to a whisper, then faded away entirely. I have never practised meditation, but there is a goal in Buddhist practice of achieving a condition of no-mind, a state of being free of thought, and I seemed to have found my way there by accident. I certainly learned to be at ease with myself in the years I spent at Penlan, but it was not by knowing myself better – it was by forgetting I was there. I had become a part of the landscape, a stone.

3. *The Sheep in the Trees*

I was sitting in my wicker chair in front of the log fire, still wearing my boots and overcoat. The candle flame guttered in the draught. The house was always draughty; it had to be to feed the fire. When the wind blew from the north, it swept down the hill and forced the smoke straight back down the chimney, and there was nothing for it but to open the front door to clear the smoke, no matter how cold it was. The floor was bare, the original clay tiles had been fired in a kiln down in the valley, along with all the bricks that were used for the estate cottages. The chequerboard of black and red was cracked and sunken now, but it was easy to mop clean of the mud that I dragged in on my heels.

When I moved in there were a handful of old paraffin lamps here, but their thin glass chimneys shattered easily and were almost impossible to replace. No one had used them in earnest in fifty years and if they are available at all it is purely for decorative purposes. So I had candles stuck in bottles, and a couple of storm lamps for when I needed to move around the house or go outside, to save spilling hot wax on my hands. Eventually, I worried that I would get eye strain from reading by candlelight, and I got hold of a hissing Sid, an old tilley lamp with original brass fittings that last saw service in the power cuts of the 1970s, and renovated that. It was a fiddle having to light the mantle with methylated spirits and keep priming it to keep the pressure up, but when I hung it from one of the ham hooks in the ceiling it would give off as much light as a 40-watt bulb, and gave a constant reassuring hiss that I learned to love.

Winters here were hard. It was not so much the cold as the long nights, and I tended to sleep early and wake with first light to minimize the hours spent sitting in darkness in forced immobility, idly tending the fire. My life revolved around that fire. My mainstay was ash, which burns well even when green. Oak is dense and heavy and needs to be well seasoned; a log of it will last for hours once the fire is hot enough to get it started. There was a stand of dead elms in the top field, long since killed off by Dutch elm disease even though down the track were a few full-grown ones that seemed to have escaped. They were still standing, barkless white skeletons, and I worked my way through them one at a time. There were a few crab apple trees in the fields, a treat that would fill the room with a scented, fruity smoke. I would use poor-quality wood too, a little at a time: birch that would spit and crackle and burn away fast, and alder that would smoulder and ooze. Everything went in the fire save for softwoods, which would coat the inside of the chimney with black sticky resin and ruin it, though I would collect basketfuls of pine cones to use as firelighters. Tending the fire became as automatic as breathing, it was my lifeline. Once I fell suddenly ill. I could feel my temperature rising fast and knew I didn't have much time. As quick as I could I brought in water and a pile of logs from the woodshed, then made up a bed by the fire and climbed in fully clothed and shivering uncontrollably. When I woke to a sunny morning on the third day, my fever had broken. I felt weak and shaken but knew that the worst was over. I had no memory at all of the whole time I had lain sick, the days were a complete blank. But the fire was still burning.

Though I missed the freedom to roam that summer brought there was a part of me that enjoyed the austerity of winter. Summertime, and the living was easy, but I didn't come here for an easy life, I came here for a hard life freely chosen, and could not complain if I found it. The stream of friends who had wanted to come for weekend visits in the summer would dry to a trickle, and then it was just me, my own devices, and the elements. The few friends who attempted a winter visit mostly discreetly decided that the next time they came back it would be when the weather was better. I don't blame them; the cold got into your bones, and no matter how many logs you threw on the fire, you never felt truly warm. The only person I regularly saw was the farmer, up to check on his sheep. In the wintertime my world shrank; as the nights drew in, I drew in too, closer to home and hearth. The hills became forbidding and life-less; the pipits and larks that teemed there in summer had abandoned them. Just a few crows, perhaps a circling buz-zard, and the occasional winter snipe that would jink away in zigzags, tower, then drop back to the ground a couple of hundred yards ahead. Everything else had headed to warmer climes, or at least to lower ground or the coast.

At home I would huddle close to the fire. There was a

coal fire in my bedroom, but there simply wasn't enough draw so the room became too smoky and I seldom used it. Instead I would keep piling on the covers until the day that the spider's web of rime on the inside of the windows, my frozen breath, was too thick to see through. Then I would move downstairs. I had a single bed on castors that I used as a sofa, and I would roll that close to the fire at night, and for the rest of the winter I would live in just the one room. The bats had left long ago to their underground winter roost, and the mice no longer troubled me; I was alone save for the little clusters of peacock and tortoiseshell butterflies that clustered in the corners of the upstairs ceilings, sleeping the winter away. I would have to keep an eye on them in the spring, to let them out when they woke.

In my first full winter at the cottage, almost on a whim, I decided to follow the birds. Not the migrants, the international travellers that had gone far south, but the moorland waders and birds of prey that had deserted my hills for the coast. I was brought up by the sea and missed it sometimes. So I walked down the hillside, crossed the river to the main road and hitched a ride north-west. First I stopped off at Aberystwyth, to watch the choughs on the sea cliffs. Choughs are our rarest and most elegant crow, glossy black with a long slender red bill and broad butterfly wings. They floated weightlessly in the updraught, calling continually, and fed in little packs on the clifftop fields. Then I headed back to the road north, to reach the estuary before nightfall. It was a cold January day, the ground was iron beneath my feet, so when I got there I booked a night in a bed and breakfast.

It was a beautiful spot. The estuary was surrounded by snow-capped peaks. Thick oak woods led you to the salt marsh, the reed beds, and pools still unfrozen in spite of the deep frost. And beyond that the mudflats, teeming with flocks of waders. Almost the first bird I saw was a glaucous gull, a rare vagrant that had followed the icy north wind down from the Arctic. Skeins of Greenland white-fronted geese lit on the marsh, gaggling and cackling, and snake-necked red-breasted mergansers dived repeatedly in the pools. A little female merlin raced back and forth along the woodland edge, never resting. Out on the flats a lone peregrine, a tiercel, was sitting on a post preening himself. He could have been the bird I watched regularly at my local eyrie. He was being, I would have to say, harried, by a male hen harrier, the palest of pastel greys save for his black wing-tips, gracefully swooping towards the falcon, over and over, then sweeping away. The peregrine seemed not to care, seemed not even to notice, he just carried on preening himself calmly, and eventually the harrier tired of this sport and went back to quartering the reed beds in search of an unwary bunting. The peregrine shook his feathers, lifted from his post and flew low and slow along the water's edge, flocks of waders scattering all around him. He dropped slightly and scooped up a red-shank. He had not even been hunting, but had virtually tripped over a free meal. There were rich pickings to be had here. At dusk, a barn owl emerged from its roost in the tangled roots of an old oak. It waited there patiently, looking out inscrutably as the sun finally set and darkness fell. Then it lifted off, pale and ghostly and totally silent, and began to hunt, criss-crossing the marsh in systematic transects in search of its prey. And with that, I left and headed back to my own eyrie in the far hills.

Deep on a winter's night I was woken by bloodcurdling screams. If I had been of a more timid disposition it might have unnerved me. The mating call of the fox – their season is the dead of winter. I got up and gently pulled aside the curtains. A pair of foxes was mating on the track right outside the cottage; in the daytime they would keep their distance, but the darkness had made them bold.

The stoat that I saw in the rain on New Year's Day I didn't see again until the following New Year's Eve. It was a fine winter morning and I was sitting out on my porch. The stoat came bouncing up the hillside like Tigger, alongside the fence. Just across my track was a boulder, and it hopped up on that, stood up on its hind legs and cocked its head from side to side, weighing me up, twitching its short black-tipped tail. And then, having seen enough, it bounded back down the field and was lost behind a turn in the fence. I remembered reading as a child of an old gamekeepers' wheeze, to call stoats by impersonating the squeals of an injured rabbit. I had absolutely no idea what an injured rabbit sounds like, but I stood up, and by sucking through my teeth made, well, a noise. And incredibly it worked. The stoat came back, reared up on to its hind legs again, and stared at me intently, as if to say: Who are you? And what on earth do you think you're doing?

Stoats are notoriously brave and inquisitive. I remember once in Sweden I took a rowboat out across a lake to a small forested island. While I was sitting on the rocky beach, a little head popped up from behind a fallen tree trunk, then disappeared, then popped up again. It was a young stoat playing peekaboo with me. I stood up to get a better view, and it ran over, nipped me on the toe of my shoe, then dashed off again. It did this three times in all before it got bored; there is no end to their boldness.

The winter season had its rewards. When I woke to a new, softer light and an unmistakable muffled silence, and knew that the first snow of winter had fallen during the night, it was like being a child again. And once or twice each winter, the wind would turn and the temperature suddenly plummet, and I would emerge into a crystal world. Every blade of grass, every strand of gossamer would be sheathed in frozen dew. My breath was a cloud of steam and the ground crunched satisfyingly beneath my feet, like I was walking on broken glass. The woods were completely silent, and completely still. It felt as though a moment in time had been frozen, and the world was holding its breath.

But the world does not stop and start. The seasons are not discrete, they have no true beginning and end, they merge into one another and overlap, all part of the flow. On a mild Christmas Day, I watched a bat circling in the valley in broad daylight, a pipistrelle flushed from hibernation by a warm snap, and was surprised by a sudden cascade of birdsong. A wren, with such a big voice for such a tiny bird. And though the birds might start singing to greet the spring before the year is out, there was one thing I could be sure of: it would snow in spring, in March or even April. It came every year without fail, that last fall of snow. The locals even had a name for it: lambing snow.

The winter thrushes had come. I liked the idea that while our summer visitors had headed off to Africa, these birds had flown all the way from the Arctic Circle and elected to spend their winters here on my hillside. They came and went through the winter; I kept thinking they were gone for good, and then they were back again in force. Scores of fieldfares, big, brash and noisy, fell from the trees to the ground and back again. The redwings, neat little birds with a glorious blood-red flash beneath their wings, were in their hundreds in the open fields. They worked their way steadily across their chosen field, all heads facing the same way.

I was walking down the track one day, watching the redwings feeding down the hill from me, when I was met by a quad bike being ridden by the farmer's niece who helped out on the farm occasionally. She pulled up and stopped for a chat. Looking out over the valley below to the far hills she said what a fine view I had up here. I commented that the landscape here was beautiful. I wouldn't really know about that, she said, and shrugged. I've never lived anywhere else. She would be marrying soon. I could see the farm she was moving to from here; she pointed it out to me. It was across the valley, only two or three miles distant, but it might as well have been another country. This would be the last time that I saw her. The farmer, her uncle, had also spent every night of his life on this hillside. He had never been to England, not thirty miles away as the crow flies. He went to Cardiff once, to get his teeth fixed. Didn't like it.

While we were talking, something slipped out of the pine woods above us, a streak of slaty grey hurtling straight towards us just an inch or two above the ground, following every undulation in the hillside. Just when it looked like collision was inevitable, it swerved around us at the last possible moment, picked up speed and crashed into the redwings feeding below. The male sparrowhawk had just used us as cover for hunting. He had passed within a foot of the farmer's niece, and she hadn't even noticed him.

These were hungry times. It wasn't long before I saw the sparrowhawk making another kill. He skated down my track from the top of Penlan Wood, and passed between the posts of the open gate towards a little flock of cock chaffinches that were feeding unaware in the field at the edge of the oak wood. At the last moment they saw him racing towards them just above the ground and lifted for the safety of the trees. The hawk flipped upwards and exe-cuted a perfect backwards roll, and when he landed on the grass there was a chaffinch seized in his talons. He stood there immobile for a few seconds as though thinking, but was in fact squeezing the life out of the bird with the force of his grasp. It seems harsh but it's a quick death. Only when his prey was still and lifeless did he begin to pluck it. Hawks prefer their prey on the ground, while most falcons specialize in birds on the wing. A peregrine will stoop on its prey from a great height and at incredible speed, killing it on impact.

I would go out walking every day, without fail, whatever

the weather. With eyes wide open I never came back disappointed. There was always something new to see; not a new species necessarily as there were only so many here to be seen, but behaviour I had never seen before, or something I had overlooked, or simply something beautiful. There was more out there than you could ever learn. If nowhere else, I would at least take a stroll down to my postbox; it was a pleasant short walk for a bad day. Down the front fields along the edge of Penlan Wood and between the old hollow oaks below. Through the gate at the bottom of the field was a crook barn, one of the oldest buildings on the estate, overhung by a row of sycamores. The barn was constructed from huge curved beams split from the trunk of an oak perhaps five hundred years ago and looked like the upturned hull of a galleon. I always peeked inside, and often there would be a tawny owl sleeping in the rafters. The place was dilapidated now, collapsing on to the rusting old farm machinery inside, though one end had been fixed up into a byre for the few cows and the pair of ponies that were kept in these fields. The fields here were steep, rocky and overgrown, no good for sheep, and wooded with oak and alder.

Down through the woods was the stream, and a crumbling stone bridge, with a keystone dating it to 1839. There was once a cart track that followed this stream all the way to the river from the hills, but it was impassable now, overgrown with brambles, bisected with fallen trees, or simply washed away. I walked upstream along what remained of the track. The dingle was deep and dark and heavily wooded, and the stream tumbled below me, one waterfall after another. Perhaps there would be a party of long-tailed tits bounding from tree to tree, swinging from slender twigs like acrobats, their tails longer than their bodies, with their camp followers behind them, treecreepers and goldcrests. The goldcrests are the smallest of all our birds. In the summer they hide away in the plantations but in the winter they emerge and somehow manage to survive its hardships. Perhaps I would see a sparrowhawk skimming the treetops, surfing the canopy in search of the flocks of siskins that fed on the alder cones. And that was enough.

Finally I came to a gate, and there by the gatepost was my postbox. I say postbox, but it was actually an old ten-gallon whitewash drum salvaged from my woodshed, perched on a couple of breeze-blocks, its lid kept on with a boulder. This was the point at which the lanes came closest to me; they went on to three more farmhouses, then petered out altogether. There was a bridge here too, in far better repair than my forgotten bridge in the woods. Come the spring, the grey wagtails would be nesting in a niche in this bridge. If I had any post I would sit on the wall of the bridge, swing my heels over the gushing stream below, and read my letters there.

If it was pouring with rain, I would make do with my trip to the postbox; I could make it there and back in little over half an hour if I rushed. But usually I would spin out my walk for an hour or two longer. In winter I tended to stay low, where there was a modicum of shelter. Most often I retraced my steps along the old cart track by the stream, back to the lost bridge. Squirrels would be chasing each other, skittering through the trees. At the bridge the stream divided into two around a rocky island. Long ago a massive oak had fallen, across both branches of the stream, island and all. Its moss-covered trunk was just a racetrack for the squirrels now, a short cut from bank to bank. Out of the four-foot-wide stump of the fallen oak grew an almost full-sized beech tree, the only beech in this wood. Before I was even born a jay had brought its prize here and secreted the seed of a beech in the crown of the oak, cached for the winter. But the jay had never returned, lost to a sparrowhawk perhaps, and the beech had taken root and grown into the hollow heart of the oak, finally bursting it open.

Over the fern-draped, crumbling masonry of this bridge was a magical world. A whole row of fields here had been bought up long ago, only to be abandoned. The first of these was completely encircled by woods, it was like a forest clearing. It was boggy and waterlogged now, the grass grew in waist-high tussocks, and it was being invaded by bracken and scrub, mostly birch, always the first on the scene. In spring this field would be filled with common spotted orchids, the only place I ever found them here. The woods on the far side of the field were a jungle of impenetrable scrub and rhododendrons that teemed with life. Badger trails emerged from under the scrub and spread across the field in every direction, but I never managed to trace them back to their sett hidden somewhere within the wall of vegetation. There were more abandoned fields downstream beyond the alder woods to the east of this clearing, just as unkempt but more exposed. The farmhouse looked out over some of these fields, and it must have been hard for the farmer to be confronted daily by land so blatantly in need of sheep.

Mostly I stayed in the first of these fields; it felt like my own special place and was the favoured haunt of the winter woodcock. As I walked around the field, they would flush from beneath my feet. They were mysterious, wise-looking birds, with their steep foreheads and long straight bills that they held pointed almost straight downwards as they flew. I never saw them on the ground, their camouflage was so effective, their mottled russet browns a perfect facsimile of dead bracken. The second they touched down they simply disappeared. They trusted this camouflage implicitly too; they only flushed when there was a serious risk they would be trodden on. Often their wings would brush against me as they rose; hundreds of times I must have unknowingly walked within inches of them.

On my first winter at the cottage there were more wintering woodcock than there ever have been since, yet though I flushed them on every walk it was months before I finally saw one grounded. I was walking on the eastern side of my mountain. Here the flank of the mountain is almost sheer and there are great views of the river far below, though in the summer the bracken grows head-high and you see nothing. There are just a few precarious sheep trails along this hillside, and it feels as though if you slipped you would roll all the way to the bottom. I was picking my way along one of these trails on my way to one of my local badger setts, wanting to check if they had emerged from their slumbers yet. And then I caught a glint at my feet. It was an eye, and what I had seen was my own reflection moving in a shiny black eye. I leaned in closer. The eye was a perfect globe, and in it I could see the entire valley in miniature. Painstakingly, around this shining eye, I was able to reconstruct the shape of a bird in the litter of dead bracken. And then it suddenly flushed, without apparent alarm, only to drop back to the ground fifty yards ahead. It could have been five yards, but still I would never have found it again. It struck me that in all my walks on my hill, I only ever flushed woodcock here on the eastern side, even though there were lots of other places all around the fringes of the hillside that seemed on the face of it equally suitable. There was a certain logic to it. Woodcock are neither day-birds nor night-birds; they are crepuscular, creatures of the half-light, active only around dawn and dusk. At nightfall, these eastern slopes would be the first places to fall into a deep enough shadow for them to rise, and in the very early morning would be the first places on the hill to become light enough for them to wake and begin their inscrutable cycle once again.

My first two winters at Penlan were relatively mild. There may have been weeks of snow in total, but there were thaws between the snowfalls. It was the third winter that was the killer. The snow would drift down the hillside in the night, and when I opened my back door in the morning I would be faced with a waist-high wall of snow that I would have to break my way through. The top two inches of the water in my water-butts would have frozen solid, and I would smash my way through the ice with a half-brick before filling my water jugs for the day. The jugs would have to be completely immersed or else they would be filled with the detritus that floated on the surface, so I would plunge my arm into the icy water and my hand would instantly turn numb. It would wake me up for the day. Being snowed in was not really a problem for me; by this time I was pretty much self-sufficient, and in my larder I had stored nearly a year's worth of vegetables and preserved foods.

Hitchhiking up from Abergavenny that winter, I got a lift with an elderly hill farmer with a long white beard that reached almost to his waist. He proudly professed himself a communist, and reminisced for a while about the glory days of the miners' strike. But before long he turned to matters closer to hand – the struggle to make a living out of rearing sheep on these godforsaken hills. He told me about the winter of '47, the worst winter in living memory. The snow fell so hard and fast and deep, and stayed so long, he said, that the farmers could not get out to tend to their flocks. And when the thaw finally came, months later, and they could at last reach the high fields, they found their dead sheep tangled in the topmost branches of the trees.

I was snowed in for nearly six weeks that winter. Each day I would dig a path out to my woodpile and chop wood. It was good to keep myself active and, as they say, a log fire warms you twice: once when you chop the logs; and again when you burn them. In a way I exulted in it. In my ramblings I seldom saw anyone at all, not even in the distance, though it could happen, and from time to time it did. But it felt liberating to wake in the morning and know that today there was no chance whatsoever that I would see anyone, nor tomorrow either. I was revelling in the experience of isolation and remoteness; more isolation, more remoteness, felt like a good thing. An uninhabited Scottish island, that would be good. The wilderness of northern Canada. Or Siberia, the Siberian taiga, why not? Deeper. Further.

The snow was too deep for me to go far from home, but each time there was a fresh fall of snow overnight I would walk around the fields just beside the cottage to see what the night had brought. If the daytime was for me and the birds, the night-time was for the mammals whose lives I seldom touched. I would have seen them more if I'd had a car and driven around the lanes at night, but seeing an animal pinned in your headlights is not what I call watching. The snow preserved an imprint of all I had missed in the hours of darkness, the wanderings of my local foxes, and more. The classic mammal of mid-Wales is the polecat, a handsome spectacled ferret. This was their heartland, and they were more common here than anywhere, yet I very seldom saw them. Partly, I think they preferred the other side of the river where there was a huge warren of rabbits, their main prey, but mostly it was because they were shy, and active almost entirely at night. Their preferred habitat was reputedly the hinterland where the hill farms met the moor, a precise description of where I lived, in other words, and the first one I ever saw conformed almost perfectly to this stereotype: he was bounding along the top of the very drystone wall that separated the topmost field from the bracken-covered moorland above. He looked back over his shoulder at me, then skipped on, leaped over a stile effortlessly, and was lost to view in the cover of a nearby stand of larches. Yet though seeing one was a special occasion, once

I could read the signs I would find their trails everywhere, in snow and in mud.

But if I could not get out to see my birds while I was snowed in, I could still bring the birds to me. On the east side of the cottage was a big old fruit tree with branches that reached almost to the ground. I never knew what kind of fruit tree because it never bore me a single fruit. From January onwards the bullfinches would arrive and almost tenderly nip off every bud, stretching out slowly, sedately even, as they worked their way steadily through the tree's bounty. I didn't mind, I could forgive a bullfinch anything, they are such handsome birds with their black hoods and rosy breasts. To be honest, I doubt the tree would have fruited anyway, for beside this tree were the dead remains of a second, and I think it would have needed this second tree for its fruit to germinate. It was on the stump of this dead tree that I put my bird table, just a few feet away from the slotted window in the east wall of my living room.

The birds were incredibly quick to take advantage of this new food supply. Within a day of my first putting out food it had been found by great and blue tits, by robins and chaffinches. Then came the tiny coal tits from the pinewoods. A pair of nuthatches arrived: dapper, long-billed birds like miniature woodpeckers, the only bird that can walk head first down a tree trunk. They would dart on to the nut-feeder, sometimes landing upside down, and send the smaller birds scattering. With their neat black eye-stripes they looked like little highwaymen, and for a short time at least they ruled the roost. Then came the local pair of great-spotted woodpeckers, much bigger birds altogether. At first they didn't seem to know what to do, they had simply followed the little birds in to see what the fuss was about, and would just pick idly at the rotten log I had left out for them. But eventually they found my offering and made it their own. It was a pleasure to sit at my window and watch them demolishing my nut supply from such close range.

More visitors came. Towards the end of the winter when the seeds had all gone from the alder cones, the feeder would be invaded by troupes of hungry siskins. Squirrels that had woken early from their winter sleep would join the birds, and field mice too. A pair of marsh tits arrived, and a pair of willow tits. Marsh and willow tits look almost identical; there are subtle differences, but the differences between individuals can be greater than that between species. I could spend hours trying to work out who was who. Their habits vary though; marsh tits nest in any tree hole they can find, like most tits, while the willow tit is the only one that excavates its own nesting hole. With their tiny beaks they need very soft wood, so they tend to live in the wet and boggy alder woods, where there is rotten wood everywhere. They fill a different niche, and occupy different territories. And like other birds that look very similar, such as willow warblers and chiffchaffs, they have quite distinctive calls. It was through their calls that I finally learned to tell them apart, and in time I could recognize each of the four individual birds. The marsh tits took over the cotoneaster by my porch and worked their way through its berries; none of the other birds would touch them, not even the barely distinguishable willows. And every time I opened my front door the marsh tits would scold me loudly with their *chickadee* call.

There were some notable absentees. The bird tables in the village were dominated by greenfinches, but only a single one ever found its way to mine. Even closer at hand, down at the farm, the barns were raided by gangs of chattering house sparrows, but again only one single wanderer ever found its way to my table. A slight difference in altitude can change the whole ecology of a place; it could be another country. Down by the river the collared doves cooed, but I never once saw one up at Penlan. There were hedgehogs down on the valley floor too, but my cottage was above the invisible barrier for them as well.

The cold weather brought the birds in droves; they thronged to the table. Blackbirds and song thrushes, much shyer here than in the parks and gardens of the city, magpies and jays that dived in from the cover of the fruit tree, the new kings. Dunnocks picked in the snow for fallen morsels, and the garden wrens that usually ignored the table joined in too. The most surprising visitor was a treecreeper, a tiny mouse-like bird with a unique feeding style. Starting at the bottom of a tree, they work their way up the trunk in spirals, with little jerky hops, winkling out microscopic insects from the bark with their needle-thin bills. When they reach the crown they fly down to the bottom of the next tree and start again. They can work their way through an entire wood doing this, and they never pause to rest because their prey is so tiny. Little creatures like these must eat constantly to keep their energy up, like the common shrews that I sometimes found in my woodshed picking through my wood supply for insects, in a constant state of high excitement. It is the tiniest birds that are most vulnerable in the cold weather, not because they freeze but because they starve. The treecreeper took to the peanut-feeder, but its feeding style was ingrained; it would start at the bottom and work its way up in spirals.

So while the world around me was frozen and still under its deep blanket of snow, around my cottage was a hive of activity. It helped make the experience of being snowed in feel not like a chore but a privilege, a holiday. I wonder how many birds made it through that hard, hard winter solely because of my intervention. I could spend hours each day sat by my narrow slotted window watching their comings and goings, their battles for supremacy. But every now and then I would have to leave my post and stand by my fire, slowly turning, because in this cold the fire can burn your front while your back still freezes.

Inevitably, the sparrowhawks found the table too; such a congregation of birds would not go unnoticed for long. Whenever I looked out at the table and found it bare of life, I knew it was because the hawks were close at hand. One morning when I went out to replenish the food supply, I surprised the female lurking in the depths of the fruit tree. She burst out of the tree, with a clatter that would have done justice to a woodpigeon. Her wings clapped once above her back, and once below. On the downstroke her wings flicked the topmost strand of the sheep-fence that topped my drystone wall, and set it zinging. Then she raced down the front field in alarm, jinking wildly like a panicked snipe. Sparrowhawks live by the element of surprise; I don't think she much liked having the tables turned for once.

Eventually the thaw came. I felt as though I had been through a rite of passage; I had experienced the worst that the elements could throw at me, and come through it unscathed. I looked forward to getting out and resuming my rambles, seeing how the wildlife had coped with the hard times just gone, but I hadn't run out of anything I couldn't manage without. I didn't need to rush to town to replenish my stocks. Town could wait. A bit more alone time would do me no harm at all.

The sun was starting to set. I wrapped up warm and left the cottage, walking down the hill past the old crook barn, over the old bridge, and to my secret clearing in the woods. I had my own personal bench here. Twin oaks had grown too close together; as their canopies reached for the light they leaned away from each other so their trunks formed the shape of a V. Their roots had entwined and meshed together and made a comfortable seat, and this is where I stopped and waited. As the skies began to darken the first flock of redwings flew in, at least two or three hundred of them. They seemed to fly in perfect synchrony so their brilliant red underwings flashed on and off in unison. They were roosting in the jungle on the far side of the clearing, but they didn't settle yet, they circled above the trees. More flocks arrived from every direction, in their hundreds. They must have been coming from miles away, from tens of miles away, until there were thousands of birds converging into one massive flock. They spiralled up into the sky, swelled into a huge bubble that suddenly burst, and scattered. They twisted and turned, shape-shifting, rising, falling, assembling, dispersing. Anyone who has seen the incredible massed aerial displays of starlings at their winter roosts will know the sight; this was like that but with added colour. It was an awesome spectacle; there were moments that made me want to gasp like people do at the grand finale of a firework display. And that is just what it was like; as the flock burst into a sudden explosion of crimson I could have been in a ringside seat at my own private firework show. Finally the last light faded away and the birds all settled into the trees. And then I left them, and trudged back up the hill in the darkness to where I hoped my fire was still burning so I could warm my bones.

4. *My Familiar*

The totemic bird of mid-Wales is the red kite. They are stunning, graceful birds with a wingspan greater than a buzzard's, perhaps five feet across. Their narrow black-and-white wings have a characteristic kink, their little pigeon-like heads are pale grey, and their breasts and that distinctive forked tail are a glorious rufous orange. They sail effortlessly on the updraught, constantly flexing and torquing their tails, a rudder to finesse their every movement. We are lucky to have them; they were brought back from the brink of extinction. It is thought that every one of them may be descended from a single female that clung to life here in my hills. Formerly they were widespread; notoriously they once long ago scavenged the rubbish tips of London, like the black kites that still feed on the rubbish tips of India in their thousands today. But centuries of persecution pushed them ever back, until they retreated to their last stand in the fastness of these hidden valleys. It is easy to understand why they were so vulnerable: when you see one floating by, as often as not it will approach and circle directly over your head to get a better look at you, in spite of all those generations of harassment. It was curiosity that killed the kite.

But the kites were silent birds, unlike the buzzards and ravens that called constantly and formed the soundtrack to my life in the hills. Both live here in population densities perhaps greater than anywhere else in the world. On clear, sunny days there would often be more than a dozen buzzards circling overhead, mewling and bickering like drunks at a wedding. When it was overcast or raining they would hunch in the trees or on fence posts as if sulking. Their staple diet was the carrion of dead sheep, but they were opportunistic feeders – they would eat whatever they could find. Often when I woke they would be out in the front field looking for any worms that had emerged in the night. I have seen them hovering almost like a kestrel, though with much less grace, then dropping into the grass to catch a vole; and they will kill a bird as large as a crow, and even kill a rabbit if they can catch it. I have only once seen a buzzard turn up its beak at the opportunity of a free meal.

I was sitting on my doorstep in the morning sun with my chain file, methodically sharpening my saw, when I noticed something crawling up the hillside towards me. It was a grey squirrel, but its head was swollen, its eyes bulging, and it appeared to be losing control of its limbs. I hadn't realized that myxomatosis could affect squirrels; or perhaps this was not myxomatosis but an equivalent squirrel disease. It couldn't support its weight; it was dragging itself up the hill on its belly, but it seemed absolutely determined and it never paused in its struggle. It was a pitiful sight. A buzzard flew up from the wood and perched in a tree above the squirrel, shaking its tail as it settled like they always do. I recognized this bird from its markings, it was one of the pair that nested in Penlan Wood. It flew down to the ground beside the squirrel and peered at it closely, and I thought it was curtains for the squirrel. But the buzzard lifted and flew back to the wood; it must have sensed that something was not right. The squirrel carried on, painfully slowly, irrevocably. Just over the track was an old ash, and there was a hollow in that ash right at ground level. The squirrel crawled into the shelter of that hole, from which it would never emerge.

Buzzards are raggedy, untidy birds; every time they make a move they seem to lose another feather. You could come back from any walk with a hatband full of buzzard feathers. The ravens are much cooler customers altogether. They get a bad press, because they are black and feed on carrion, I suppose, though in some cultures they are revered, as the bird that brought us the sun, or even as our creator. They are thought to be the most intelligent of all birds, as intelligent as dogs. They mate for life and have a wide range of vocalizations, the most sophisticated communication skills of any bird. The most familiar call is a deep cronk; if you see a raven this is what you will probably hear. Because if you can see a raven you can be sure it will have seen you first, and the cronking is actually a very mild alarm call. The other constant call is a beautiful bell-like ringing tone that you hear when the birds are out of sight, the contact call between a pair.

The ravens are monolithic black slabs that float across the hillside with scarcely a wing-beat; they are massive. With their straight wings, their diamond-shaped tails, their long necks and shaggy heads, they look like Maltese crosses silhouetted against the sky. As they fly they repeatedly fold their wings tight against their body, flip on to their backs and fly upside down, first one bird then the other. This stunning display seems almost joyous, as if the birds are rejoicing in the freedom of the skies. It is described as a spring courtship display, but I have seen it in every month of the year. They almost infallibly come in twos, and the pair remains together all year round, always close, always loyal. Except for when they are followed by a trail of their young they are not generally social members of the crow family, such as the rooks and the jackdaws, or the choughs on the cliffs. Although one August when I walked to the top of my mountain I found a meet of perhaps twenty-five birds above the summit, not just flipping on to their backs but performing complete rolls, then dropping like stones to the ground and swooping up at the last possible moment. This mysterious gathering continued for hours as I watched from a distance, awestruck by their total mastery of the air and wondering at the purpose of it all.

Magpies are known for these occasional inscrutable parliaments too. They are not social birds either – the rhyme only goes up to seven, after all – but occasionally they will assemble in much larger numbers for reasons not fully understood. I saw such a meeting just once in my time in the hills. There were five birds in a circle on the ground, all facing inwards and hopping around awkwardly as if they were not sure quite what to do. All around them in the trees and bushes near by was an outer circle of nearly twenty watching birds, like the audience at a gladiatorial contest.

I found the local raven nest during my first winter, before I had moved into Penlan full-time. On the steep bracken-covered eastern flank of my hill are a series of small copses. Some are natural – alder woods that follow the trickle of a stream down the mountainside – but evenly spaced between them are several small stands of ornamental conifers, planted long ago for the benefit of the view from the big house far away across the valley. The Victorians had a habit of introducing features to the landscape that would be seen to their full advantage only by their grandchildren, or great-grandchildren. In a way you have to admire their confidence; they must have thought their time would never end. That winter I picked my way across the hillside while the bracken was dead and brown, exploring each of the little copses in turn. And high up in the tallest cedar in the biggest of these copses I found the nest. It was vast; it looked like generations of ravens must have added to it, but in fact I later discovered that it was relatively recent. They had previously nested for years across the river and further up-valley, but the site had been visible from the road and drunks from the local pub had one night decided to take pot-shots at the nest with their air rifles.

When spring came I began to watch the birds at the nest. Ravens are among the first birds to breed; they will work on their nest through February and then begin to lay in early March, when the hills where they live are often still streaked with drifts of snow. Birds time their nesting so that the weeks when the nest is full of hungry mouths to feed will coincide with the time their food supply is at its most plentiful. For ravens this meant lambing season, when the fields would be full of stillborn lambs and afterbirths. Whether or not the increased adoption of lambing sheds will affect the density of their population remains to be seen.

From the ridge of the hill I could look straight down into the nest at the sitting bird brooding her eggs, far enough away that I did not disturb her. But I preferred to watch from below. At the track where the moorland met the highest fields, I would sit on the stile where I had seen my first polecat and look up at the nesting copse. The male would come sailing in across the valley, calling repeatedly. He was so big that his arrival seemed to make the hillside shrink around him. He would settle in a tree in the adjacent copse and the sitting female would fly out to him. And then he would sing to her, a quiet, gentle trilling song that you would never expect to hear from a member of the crow family, and they would touch beaks tenderly. After that they would launch themselves from the trees and circle together, each flipping over in turn, their calls ringing out across the valley. The pair raised their five young successfully that year. Once they were on the wing they spread themselves over the hillside trees, calling for food, but soon they began to follow their parents everywhere in a long line, a crocodile in the sky. Wherever I went I would see them trailing after the adults, trying to copy their every move, discovering their domain.

It was late in February, the tail end of the following winter, and there was excitement in the air; there was a palpable feeling that everything in my world was preparing for change. A pair of ravens was displaying continually over Penlan Wood; one bird would fly down and pluck a twig, then circle around holding it proudly in its beak, while the other bird seemed driven to transports of delight, calling excitedly and not just rolling but plummeting down into the trees just like the displaying sparrowhawks. There was a third bird too, always watching from a distance; every time it approached a little too close the pair would chase it off angrily. I checked the pair in the hillside cedar, but they were in their place; these were different birds. I suspected they might be last year's young that had not wandered too far from their birthplace; a couple that had paired off and an unmated male. I wondered if they planned to nest in the wood right on my doorstep, even though my sparrowhawks seemed none too keen on having them around, but once they became serious about nest-building I saw them daily ferrying sticks downhill towards the stream.

Over the course of a week I kept a lookout for the nesting site in the streamside woods, but couldn't locate it. Once breeding began in earnest the pair's constant display flights came to a halt and I would see the male alone flying straight and purposeful down into the wooded valley. And it was only when the female started sitting that the reason I had failed to find the nest became apparent; I had seen the nest almost straight away but had taken it for a wood-pigeon's, it was so tiny. The old nest in the cedar was the size of a bale of hay, while this one was so small the sitting female overhung it, head, tail and sides too. The nest was about thirty feet up in a slender birch alongside my clearing across the old bridge, and wisps of wool lining trailed beneath it. It seemed such an unlikely location for a bird of the high crags and the open hills; but these birds were beginners, if my hunch was correct, and this was their first attempt. As I looked up and saw the bird sitting there, squeezed into her paltry nest, she saw me too and flew up, circling above the woods and calling over and over again. The male joined her within seconds, and the two birds took out their anger on an unfortunate buzzard that happened to be passing.

I would go down to my bench on the far side of the clearing, a suitable distance away to keep an eye on them without disturbing them, and the spare bird would always be in the vicinity too, a fellow watcher, though every time he drifted too close the mated birds would be on his tail at once. The pair managed to successfully rear their own brood of five young that year, even though it seemed miraculous that all those birds could fit into such a tiny nest. They did leave the nest before they could fly, but it didn't matter, they just draped themselves around the canopy of the little birch, like flags on a pirate ship, calling repeatedly for their parents to bring them food. And I was there as they took their first faltering flights.

Coming down off the hill one sunny afternoon I noticed something big and black on the track by my cottage. At first I thought it must be one of the farm cats that sometimes wandered up this far. They lived in the barns around the farmhouse and I had no idea how many there were; I doubt the farmer did either. The most I ever saw at one time was thirteen of them waiting outside the farm door at feeding time. But as I approached I saw that this was no cat but a raven sitting motionless at the side of the track. I got closer and closer, expecting it to flush, but it never did, it just stayed in place, immobile save for the occasional blink. There was obviously something seriously wrong. They say that if a bird is so ill or badly hurt that it loses its fear of man, then it is too ill to survive. This bird didn't flinch at all as I stretched down and picked it up. It was so big that my hands only reached partway around its breast, and its pickaxe bill was bigger than my thumb, although with their hollow bones birds are always much lighter than they appear. I could see no sign of injury, and it looked in perfect condition, but it didn't struggle at all in my hands. There was not the least sign of life in it save for the blink of its eye. A hippoboscid, a wingless louse fly, scuttled out from under its feathers, then disappeared again. I had always taken ravens to be jet black, but this close up the bird was two-tone, its plumage shone with a glossy metallic sheen in purple and green. It felt like an incredible honour to have such a beautiful wild creature in my hands.

I felt sure this was the third bird, the watcher. Perhaps he had been harried to exhaustion by the relentless mobbing of the mated pair, I thought. I carried him into the cottage and placed him carefully in a cardboard box with a bowl of water while I stoked up the fire and put on the kettle. I sat by the fire with the still, silent bird at my feet, and fantasized: I would nurse him gently back to health and he would become a wild companion. Not my pet but my familiar, my connection with the natural world around me. It was just a fantasy, though, and I knew that I had to do what was in the best interests of the bird. When I had finished my cup of tea I covered the box and left the bird to rest while I set off down the hillside to the lanes and the telephone box. I called the doctor at the field centre; luckily he was in and he arranged to meet me in a couple of hours at the bridge by my postbox, where he would pick up the bird and drive it to an animal-rescue centre. There they had the experience in caring for injured birds that I lacked, and I knew this would be the raven's best chance for survival.

When I got home from my round trip of perhaps an hour and a half the raven had not moved at all; his prospects did not look good. As I opened the box to check on him he looked up at me with a perfectly round black eye that revealed no trace of fear. I covered him again and set back off down the hill carrying the box. It was turning into a busy day for me. As I sat on the wall of the bridge waiting for the doctor to arrive, I heard a faint scratching of claws from inside the box, the very first movement the bird had made in all the hours he had been with me. The doctor arrived and took him away, and I made my way back up the hill, a little regretful perhaps, even though I knew I had done the right thing. What happened next I would find out only later. The doctor stopped off at his home in the village to have his dinner before the long drive to the rescue centre. When he came back to the car an hour later he heard sounds coming from inside the boot, so decided to check on the bird before starting the journey. As he lifted the lid of the box, the raven sprang into the air. It circled the village once to get its bearings, then headed straight back in the direction of Penlan. The most likely explanation is that he had been concussed, and just needed a little time to recover.

It was dusk and I was trailing my way up the front field dragging a heavy fallen log. I would seldom arrive back at the cottage unencumbered as I always needed fresh wood. I heard a raven calling behind me. It was unmistakably a raven, but like no raven I had ever heard before; this bird sounded angry, or even scared. I looked back and saw him coming up the hillside towards me, flying low, weaving and swerving. Directly above him was his persecutor, a pale brown male goshawk with his long legs stretched out beneath him, following the raven's every move from just a few feet over his head. The hawk dropped and slammed into the raven's neck. Though there was only a short distance between them, the raven was visibly jolted by the impact, despite the fact he was the bigger bird. The hawk lifted and struck again a second time, and then a third. He didn't fold his wings and swoop for the attack as you might expect, but instead gracefully raised his wings until they touched one another directly over him, like an avenging angel. The mated pair of ravens flew up from the streamside to see what the commotion was about and perched in Penlan Wood at the very tops of the two tallest Christmas trees, where the stars go. The frail tops sagged under their weight and the two birds bobbed and swayed like boxers entering the ring. I didn't know if it was their arrival that frightened off the hawk, or if he saw me watching transfixed, my log still in my hands, but he sheered away and raced for cover. Game over; and it was a game too, as the hawk had no serious intention of killing the raven.

The crows and the birds of prey live in a constant state of war. The instinct to mob a predator is so imprinted on

birds that differing species of birds of prey will even relentlessly mob one another. In the battle between the crows
and the hawks the crows will often win on tactics, for they
are much brighter animals altogether. The hawks do not
live on their wits; with their incredible eyesight and their
bodies designed for speed and lightning-fast reactions
they must live out their lives in a whirling rush of pure
sensation.

That year I was doing some work for the estate in the
hilltop wood, the long plantation of mainly Scots pine
above my top field. The wood was twenty years old now,
and it had passed the thicket stage and needed thinning
out. I was to fell every fifth row of trees, stripping them of
branches and foliage and leaving their trunks to be collected later. It was slow, laborious work with only my
cranky old chainsaw that would keep stalling on me, but
there was no rush to finish the job, I just went up there as
and when the mood took me. Most days I would stroll up
the hill with my saw and petrol can for an hour or two. It
was peaceful up there, at least until I started my chainsaw.
I began to notice that every time I felled a tree and looked
up at the newly revealed patch of sky, there seemed to be a
raven circling directly overhead, drawn by curiosity, I supposed, to the noise I was making. I saw the raven whenever
I was out at my woodpile too. I would be out there chopping wood every day the sun shone; my fire seldom went
out and I constantly needed to keep the woodshed stocked,
in readiness for the long wet spells that could come at any
time. Almost as soon as I struck the first blow with my axe
the raven would appear overhead, circling and swooping

low, and calling, calling. Not the usual cronk you hear when a raven sees you but the contact call. His bell-like ringing would echo each stroke of my axe.

I was out at the woodpile again, weighing the axe in my hands. It was not a normal chopping axe but a big heavy splitting axe. Smaller logs I could split in a single swing, but the bigger rounds from the trunk of a tree took more work. I rolled them up on to my chopping block and drove a notch into them with the axe. Then I put a thick iron wedge into the split and hammered it in using the heel of the axe as a sledgehammer. It was satisfying work. The clang it made was a surprising facsimile of the calls of the raven above. I looked up at the circling raven. He was closer than ever, swooping down to me and calling more insistently than ever, as if he were trying to tell me something. I began to wonder if he wanted me to follow him, so I lay down my axe and set off after him.

He led me right along the top edge of Penlan Wood, flying low just ahead of me, and he kept looking over his shoulder to check I was still with him. At the end of the wood I clambered over a barbed-wire fence and down into the steep fields beyond. After a short distance further the raven stopped leading me on and circled directly above me. I looked around me and finally saw a skein of white in a fold in the hillside, a long-dead sheep that I hadn't noticed before because it was nearly hidden in the bracken. As I approached two ravens flew up, then four carrion crows. Finally, two magpies took to the trees, chattering angrily at being disturbed, and my raven flew down to the feast. I don't know whether he was inviting me to join him for lunch, or simply using me to drive away his competitors, but either way he made me laugh. My familiar.

Unlike most birds, male and female ravens don't differ in size or plumage, and unlike the buzzards, for example, they don't have markings that vary from bird to bird. To our eyes they are indistinguishable. I didn't really even know for sure that the injured bird I had found was a male, I was just making an educated guess. It was a measure of how far immersed I was becoming in this little patch of wild country that I called my own that I was no longer seeing birds as representatives of their species, but as often as not would have an idea of their histories, how old they were, where they had been born, where they were nesting, where their territories and hunting ranges began and ended. My methods may not always have been scientifically rigorous, but then I was not attempting a scientific study, rather an experiment in life.

The raven pair never came back to their birch-tree nest in the woods. It was only to be expected; this was a starter home, after all. Ravens are long-lived birds, and I like to imagine them now as a venerable old pair living in a mansion, a stately pile on a mountainside crag. The big old nest in the cedar was still used, year after year, so there were always ravens close at hand for me to watch. My world would have been a poorer place without them. And as for my familiar, well, over the course of a year he became gradually less and less familiar. His social visits became steadily more and more sporadic until the following winter when they ceased altogether. And that was as it should be; this was a majestic wild bird, a creature of the skies, not a pet. I hope and trust that he found a mate of his own in time, and I wish him a life free of persecution by marauding goshawks. And when I am out walking in the hills and a raven comes sailing by that little bit closer than usual, I like to imagine that, just possibly, it could be him.

5. Restless Creatures

Spring came to me like a liberation, the first gulp of air after diving too deep. Though I enjoyed facing the challenges that winter brought, by the tail end of the season I began to yearn for the first signs of change. I had my own personal marker for the new season; not the arrival of the summer migrants, the first swallow or the first cuckoo, but earlier than that. I waited impatiently for it. It came to me in the early dawn, a plangent peal that rippled up the hillside from the fields below, then trailed away to nothing. It was such an evocative sound for me, it transported me instantly back to when I was a boy. My childhood haunt was the local marshes, and my habit was to rise at first light to get there before the dog-walkers. In the winter vast flocks of dunlin wheeled over the mudflats, and chevrons of little black brent geese would settle on the salt marsh. In spring the hares would be boxing in the fields. But always, always, there would be the curlews.

The curlews that came to these hills each year to nest never failed me; they always returned in the second week of March. I knew that the hard times were not really over yet, and there would still be more snow, but from this point on change was in the air, there would be new arrivals almost daily. The curlews didn't just always arrive in the same week each year, they always returned to the same place too, and on the day I first heard one I would always go to see them. Down the hill and past the old crook barn, through the woods and over the bridge. Across the overgrown fields where the winter woodcock hid I reached the lanes. By the crossroads on the lanes were a series of flat fields that once were boggy and almost unworkable. Years ago, many pairs of curlews would nest here, and many pairs of lapwings too. That was before the farmer who owned the land dug trenches and put in land drains to dry out the soil, then ploughed and reseeded these fields to make better grazing.

The curlews, the biggest of our waders, with their impossibly long decurved bills designed for finding food in deep mud, didn't much like this improved grassland, and usually just one pair would remain here to breed, and one pair of noisy lapwings too. Yet still the curlews came here to gather each year before they dispersed to the hills, and I could expect to see twelve or fifteen of them together, taking turns to rise into the air and display, making their curling calls and that liquid song so beautiful it can bring a tear to the eye. And as for the many lapwings that used to come here to breed, each year fewer and fewer of them seemed to come. At first there might be perhaps fifteen of them displaying among the curlews, but now, apart from that last remaining pair that clung on here to breed, they hardly came at all. I knew of nowhere else in the area where they remained. They are one of the farmland birds that have been worst affected by agricultural changes, a creature rapidly disappearing from our landscape.

Long before the international migrants began to appear,

while the winter parties of redwings and fieldfares were still moving north, our own internal migrants were returning from the low ground and the coast. The hills, desolate all winter, were suddenly filled with an abundance of skylarks and meadow pipits. It would be months before the moors fell silent again. And the peregrines were back on their eyrie. They used to frequent the steep hill directly across the river valley from me, whose crags I could see looming above the oak wood. It was an unusual nesting site; the crags were too accessible for the falcons' tastes and they preferred to make their home in an old ravens' nest in the plantation below. If the peregrines had still nested there I would have seen them daily, but now I would see them from the cottage only a few times a year. When the big commercial quarry up-valley was abandoned, the pair moved straight on to the high cliffs there, less convenient for me, but much more suitable for them.

It was about a two-hour walk for me to go and visit them, but for peregrines it was worth it, and all through spring and right into summer, when the young took to the wing, a weekly walk up to the old quarry would be a part of my routine. Sometimes it is enough just to wander aimlessly, but sometimes it is good to have a destination in mind. On the hill alongside the crags was a large plantation and I would approach through the dense cover of the trees, crossing a stream that fell through the wood in a series of wild cascades. I would position myself just inside the wood and level with the eyrie, far enough away that I would not disturb them. In fact they never gave any sign of even having noticed me, as I was too far away to constitute any kind of threat. The male, the tiercel, would nearly always be in place, motionless on his buttress like a gargoyle, looking out intently over the valley far below from beneath his black helmet. Occasionally he would light out and turn a few graceful circles, his wild keening call echoing on the rocks. Immediately, the throng of jackdaws that nested at the far end of the crags and in the abandoned quarry buildings would take to the air in a cacophony of alarm. A pair of kestrels lived on these crags too, well away from the much larger peregrine falcons, and they would slip out from their nest with the utmost caution.

Whenever a bird passed close by, the peregrine would launch himself from the cliffs in pursuit. An incautious woodpigeon flew up the valley and he raced after it, following every twist and turn as it tried to make its escape, before circling back to his perch. He was not hunting, it was just a reflex. A raven loomed over the top of the crags, and the tiercel caught up with it in seconds; he flew directly beneath it, rolled on to his back, and tapped it repeatedly on its breast with a single talon. It was done with balletic poise, the peregrine seems incapable of a clumsy move. At last the female burst from the nest and raced across the valley for the hills, her wings winnowing in her hurry to find food. The tiercel circled and took his turn at the nest, and my watching was over for the day unless I decided to await the falcon's return.

A sparrowhawk raced up-valley across the river from where I was watching, near to home, and settled in the crest of a fully grown Scots pine directly opposite me. It began to drizzle with rain as I waited for her to emerge from cover. Eventually she left her perch and started to rise, to where a group of four buzzards was circling over the hillside. The hawk circled higher and higher, bypassing the buzzards and climbing far above them. The sparrow-hawk's nesting display is typically associated with sunny spring mornings. It was late afternoon and it was raining, but I had seen enough of sparrowhawks by then to know that they can be relied on to do the unexpected.

The next day I set off across the footbridge over the river to take a look at the suspected nesting site. Parties of black-headed gulls drifted far above me, all headed north, on their way from the sea to their breeding grounds in the hills. As I crossed the road I found a dead polecat, roadkill. I was surprised it hadn't been cleared away by the buzzards and crows; it looked like it had been there for a while. The place I was headed for was a pretty spot: a rocky outcrop of the hillside flanked by larch woods and capped by a little copse of mature Scots pine. As I clambered up the hillside through the greening larches I found a recently killed crow, only half-plucked, and saw the hawk soaring above the pines, her tail broadly fanned, her breast delicately barred in brown and white. After making a few circuits she folded her wings and swooped down towards the trees, then rose, then swooped again, five or six times. Eight buzzards soared over the treeline. One seemed to be trying to impersonate the hawk in its own untidy fashion, folding its wings and plunging down fifty or a hundred feet. The difference was that at the bottom of each dive was a second buzzard. The first few times the attacking bird swung away at the last moment, but finally it reached out a claw and struck home. I scrambled up rocks the last few metres to the stand of pines. It was too early in the year for nest-building, but I found two old nests in adjacent trees: broad, flattened tangles of sticks high up and close to the trunk. The purpose of the hawk's spring display is to ensure that nests are evenly distributed across the available range; this site was only half a mile or so away from the nest in Penlan Wood, and beyond Penlan the next site I knew of was a scant five hundred metres further west. It showed just how many of these hawks the hills could support. As I left, a pair of crows was relentlessly mobbing a buzzard, driving it almost to the ground. Above them all circled the sparrowhawk, watching.

On my way home I decided to take a long cut up the hill, on a well-worn sheep trail across the moor. The first pale green tendrils were emerging from the thick chestnut mat of last year's bracken. I rubbed my fingers on one of the delicate coils for that distinctive musty smell, the smell of spring on the moor. When I was halfway up the trail, a male sparrowhawk shot over the hilltop and hurtled down the sheer hillside a few feet above the ground, crossing the track just ahead of me. His wings were not outstretched but folded almost to his sides like those of a stooping peregrine. He raced down into the valley at great speed, compact and bullet-like, without apparently moving a muscle. This was not so much flight as controlled freefall. I couldn't help but note his trajectory, which led him by the shortest possible route from Penlan Wood towards the new site I had identified earlier that day. I knew that a male sparrowhawk had recently been found dead near by in the valley, beneath someone's French windows, and my suspicion was that the Penlan Wood male had filled the vacancy, and was supporting two females.

But as I followed the hawk's traverse of the hillside, I noticed something else too, a familiar-looking mound of earth protruding from the flattened remains of dead bracken, and decided to go down for a closer look. The sett was bigger and older than most others in the area, with five holes in regular use, and two more that looked abandoned now. I couldn't understand why I hadn't found this sett before; it was incredibly close to home, and it made me realize how easy it is to become a creature of habit, always following the same paths and keeping the same times. The sett I had been using for badger-watching was much further along the hill, over past the ravens' nest in the cedar, and was hard to get close to without drawing attention to myself. This would be much more suitable; I needed to cross only one field to look down over it from a distance, and if I wanted to get up close, there was a clump of alders on a patch of level boggy ground just twenty feet away which would almost always be downwind of the sett.

The badgers around here fed mostly on the farmland, but their setts were on the moor. I knew of only two setts down on the farmland, both in impenetrable thickets, while on the east and north sides of the mountain where the bracken grew tall there were setts every couple of hundred yards, all at the same altitude, about fifty yards above where the topmost fields turned to moor. They were wary animals here, and with good reason. In the wild valley to

the north of my hill, I found a sett that had been recently
dug out. On the mound of earth beside it was the skull of
a badger cub, unmistakable from the thick bony ridge
down the centre of the cranium. And walking on the lanes
one day, a Land Rover had pulled up alongside me; a hunts-
man late for the hunt and asking if I had seen or heard it.
We got to chatting and the conversation turned to badgers.
Badgers were beautiful, harmless creatures, he told me, and
he liked to kill them too. This was a country matter;
townsfolk didn't understand these things.

I didn't visit the sett that night – the scent I must have
left around their home during my inspection would have
made them too cautious – but soon I returned, approaching from behind the cover of the alder wood. I positioned
myself at the edge of the copse looking down over the sett,
my back to the trunk of a tree so that my silhouette
wouldn't stand out against the sky. Badger-watching is a
good test of one's ability to stay still. It is harder than you
would think; we are restless creatures by nature. After the
sun had set, but well before dark, a striped muzzle emerged
from the underground lair and tested the air. It disappeared
again, and I thought at first that I had been rumbled, but
then a big boar badger came barrelling out of the sett,
closely followed by two sows. They remained around their
heavily trampled arena for a while, scratching and sniffing.
Badgers move with a sinuous roll that belies their bulk. As
darkness began to fall, the boar and one of the sows set off
on separate trails, to search for earthworms in the fields
below, while the second sow remained behind and made a
great show of collecting up dead bracken as fresh bedding,

dragging bundles of it backwards into the sett. When she too had left the area I slipped away unnoticed. With luck I would get to see this year's young emerging for the first time before the end of May. By then the whole hillside would be deep in bracken, and the badgers' trails would be green tunnels that would render them as unwatchable above ground as below.

But the badgers had competition for their share of my spring evenings. Just as often I would head to my spot down the hill and over my stream. These fields had a life all their own: untrodden and ungrazed, they were rapidly returning to their natural state. There were plenty of kestrels in the hills, but I never saw them hovering over the farmland elsewhere; the close-cropped grass simply didn't support enough small mammals for them. These overgrown fields, though, were like an island of plenty for them. Cuckoos came here too, drawn I think not only by the availability of caterpillars, their preferred food, but also by the plenitude of tree pipits that launched themselves from their song posts in every scrubby tree. The call of the cuckoo can be heard for miles around, and they are much less common than it might seem. You will hear them often but see them seldom, even with their voice to guide you. Think what a rare sight they would be were they silent.

Barn owls hunted here too, attracted by the multitude of voles that tunnelled their way through the long grass. No barn owls nested on this side of the river, though I knew of two nesting sites across the valley, one in an old hollow oak and one in an abandoned barn. This was the only place they would cross the river for, and sometimes their unearthly screeching would drift up to me at the cottage from these fields. Barn owls have a completely different breeding strategy from the tawnies. The tawny will adjust its clutch size each year according to the availability of food, while the barn will produce four or five young each year without fail. In an exceptional year, all the young will survive, but in most years only the biggest and strongest will make it. My farmer's nephew once found a young owl down on the edge of these fields. He took it to the rescue centre but it was dead on arrival. It was just feather and bone, starved to death.

Now that spring had come the vast majority of the winter woodcocks had already headed back to Scandinavia for the season, but a handful remained here to breed, and it was the wondrous roding display of the woodcock that I had come here to see. I arrived at my bench earlier than I needed so that I could first listen to the evening chorus. The thicket across the clearing was dense with life; there was a whole symphony of birdsong there, an invisible orchestra. As darkness began to settle over the land, the birds started to fall silent one by one, until none was left save for the last mistle thrush. And just as he too fell silent, the male woodcock emerged and began his flight. He circled the clearing with a slow, moth-like fluttering flight. Round and round he went, flying low at about treetop level, silhouetted against the sky and continually making his twin roding call, a low frog-like croak followed by a high-pitched chirrup. He would do this every night for months, and every morning too, in his efforts to attract a mate. Unlike the Penlan sparrowhawk, he was a strictly clockwise bird. Sometimes, as he flew over the alder copse to the east of the clearing, he would pass by a second displaying bird, also travelling clockwise. This fringe of alders must have marked the territorial boundary. As well as having a subtle beauty, this bird has a mystique to it that drew me back again and again. Victorian naturalists reported that the woodcock, unlike any other bird, would transport its young to safety by carrying them between its thighs. For generations this was thought most probably to be a myth, until a century later it was reliably observed and found to be true. After watching this bird's display many times, I finally saw something that, while perhaps not as dramatic as the way it carries its young, was extraordinary enough for me. He was mid-circuit when a second bird suddenly rose from the long grass and flew straight up to him, pulling him up short. For a short while the pair danced together in the air, breast to breast, claw to claw, then they fluttered down to the ground to mate.

Not long after the curlews returned to the hills, the first of the international migrants started to arrive too. Earliest of all was the chiffchaff, arriving back before the last of the redwings and fieldfares had even set off for their nesting grounds in the countries of the north; and then the wheatear, returning to the drystone walls that flank the moor, and to the cairns on the mountaintops. There are one or two types of bird that wait until May – the swift, for example, and, last of all, the spotted flycatcher – but almost all arrive in quick succession throughout April. Their consistency over the years was astonishing; not only could they be relied on to arrive in the same order, they would also consistently arrive within a day or two of the previous year's arrival date. If the first wonder of migration is how birds manage to navigate thousands of miles back to the same tiny copse they were born in, the second is how they manage to time their journey so that they arrive back on the same day their parents did the previous year. Most of them, the woodland birds at least, I would see first in the trees along the stream on my way to my postbox, often in large groups. It would be like welcoming back old friends: the confiding pied flycatchers; the almost tropically exotic redstarts; and a whole raft of warblers. Some of them, the garden warblers and blackcaps, I would rarely see at any other time, for they are retiring birds of thick cover, the location of their territories best found by people better than me at picking out the song of individual birds from the cacophony of the dawn chorus. And once the migrants were back, there was no rest for them, it was now that the race for life truly began; to establish territories, protect them, find a mate, raise a brood. These were hectic times.

Before even the first migrant arrived a handful of our resident birds would have started breeding. The raven would be sitting on her eggs high in her lofty cedar, but at the opposite end of the spectrum of birds, the long-tailed tits would not be far behind her, the feeding parties of winter long since having broken up. On the day the curlews arrived, I found two of the tits' distinctive nests, one on the riverbank and one on the old railway track, already fully built though not yet lined. Both were in dense gorse bushes, their preferred nesting place for the protection it gives them from predators. All tits are hole-nesters, but long-tailed tits are misnamed – they are not really tits at all – and build the most elaborate and beautiful nests of any of our birds. A perfect egg-shaped ball of moss and lichen, knitted together with cobwebs and lined with up to two thousand feathers. It is a time-consuming business building a nest like this, the birds fly back and forth constantly in a fever of activity, and it's no wonder they have to start so early. The nest seems tiny, it's hard to imagine that a single bird with such a long tail could fit in there, let alone a whole brood, but they do.

The day after the curlews came, the showers began, building to a steady, relentless downpour that seemed as if it would never let up. The following day I walked to the river to find the water level had risen by seven or eight feet overnight and the long-tailed tits' gorse bush was now a green island draped with flotsam. The water never quite reached the nest but it was too late, it was abandoned anyway, before it had even been lined. The nest on the railway track was a success though, the entire brood fledged, and when the season was over curiosity got the better of me and I took the nest home to dissect. The birds had done a good job of keeping it clean; they were fastidious parents. This nest was lined with around twelve hundred feathers. There was not as much variety as I might have hoped for; the nest was located near to some pheasant-rearing pens and over eighty per cent of the lining was pheasant feathers. But there were at least sixty tawny owl feathers too, presumably from a nearby old nesting hole, and significant numbers from blackbirds, woodpigeons and curlews. It took me all afternoon to pick through and sort them, and then I laughed at myself and wondered if I had too much time on my hands.

When the breeding season began in earnest, I got to work on a weekly check of the hundred and twenty nest boxes I looked after, scattered through a sprawling trail of woods down in the foothills. It would take the whole day to visit them all. There were a couple of small alder woods on the way, and one mature mixed oak wood dotted with beeches and pines, but mostly they were hanging oak woods. These are the classic woodlands of Wales, positioned on steep rocky hillsides with the trees' trunks twisted and contorted from the elements and fighting their way through the boulders. Given the chance this woodland would cover the whole land, as it once did long ago, and the hanging, twisted woods that remain are simply the fragments that have been left untouched because they are in spots unsuitable for cultivation, too steep or too rocky or both. They have their own unique atmosphere, these hillside woods with their thick ground layer but little understorey, and there are a handful of birds that are most at home in these woods, who live here in population densities unmatched anywhere else: the wood warblers, the pied flycatchers, the redstarts. You step into the green light that filters through the canopy and are assailed by bird calls: the chinking of chaffinches and great tits; the gentle cascade of the willow warblers; and the trilling song of the wood warblers that is the defining sound of these woods, along with their call, a kind of gentle whoop that wouldn't sound out of place in a jungle. I don't like phonetic renderings of birdsongs, they never seem to me to do the bird justice; birds simply don't use our alphabet, they need one all of their own.

These woods felt totally wild; they were trackless and I never met anyone else while I was walking through them searching for the boxes one by one. I came every week for over two months, and recorded on nest-record cards the different stages of nest-building, laying dates and when the mother bird began to sit, hatching dates, the development of the young and when they fledged. I didn't keep these records only for the birds in the boxes but for any other nests I found too on my way through the woods: the robins and warblers that hid their nests in the ground layer among the bluebells; the thrushes in the hedgerows along the way; the goldcrests' tiny mossy nests suspended from the branches of a conifer; the stock doves and the buzzards deep in the woods. I have a knack for finding nests, but I'm not sure it is something I could teach; it's as if you have to think like a bird, you have to try to imagine the place that you would choose were you that bird. You have to get to know the individual preferences of different species. As you watch them from a distance, where is their attention focused? And, as you approach closer, where does their anxiety emanate from? My observations of individual birds meant the most to me personally, but these were not scientific. An incident of dramatic behaviour I had seen could well have been anomalous. Scientific validity comes from the slow accretion of small facts. It is the analysis of tens of thousands of nesting records that will reveal a population slump or a change in the distribution of a species. So this was me paying my dues.

My nesting boxes would all be in use, every last one, unless perhaps one had lost its lid during the winter. Over half of them would be occupied by pied flycatchers, stocky, handsome little birds, the male black and white, the female brown and white. They are uncommon elsewhere but in these oak woods they are the most numerous species. Their population seems to be limited not so much by the supply of food as by the availability of suitable nesting holes, so if you fill a wood with nest boxes you can double the local population. Although it is not a common bird, not even a familiar bird to those who live elsewhere, it is one of the most intensively studied of all British birds. There are two main reasons for this: the first is simply because they take so readily to nest boxes; the second is that they sit so tight. It is possible to lift the sitting bird off her eggs, check the nest, and replace her as she was. The birds seem completely unfazed by this level of intrusion, though the male may come and hop around you, calling in annoyance while you are there. A significant number of the sitting females would have been ringed in these same woods as infants, so I took down the numbers and sent them off for the record. It was all grist to the mill.

Of the remaining fifty or sixty boxes, most would have been taken by blue and great tits, in roughly equal numbers. Unlike the placid pied flycatcher, the blue tits are notorious for the struggle they put up when you lift them off their eggs, and given the chance they will jab their tiny beaks into the quick of your fingernails where it will hurt the most. A few boxes would go to the nuthatches, one or two of the boxes in the alder woods would be taken by marsh tits, and those few boxes situated on conifers might be occupied by coal tits. There would always be a couple of pairs of redstarts, although they found the standard hole size of a tit box a tight squeeze.

The nuthatches would without fail be the first to lay their eggs. These birds would naturally choose holes with larger entrances than they need, such as old woodpecker holes, and rebuild them, gathering damp soil and plastering it on so that it will dry to give them an entrance hole that is just so. With these nest boxes this was surplus to requirements, as the holes were already quite small enough for them, but the habit dies hard, and they would do their best instead to plaster the box to its tree, or plaster down its lid.

It was a pleasure to wander this trail up and down the hills and through these untouched woods each year as spring developed, the bluebells blooming and the woods burgeoning with life, while knowing that I was in some tiny way adding to the sum of human knowledge. But it was not all sunshine and bluebells and new life taking flight. In my third year of doing this survey, it rained almost every day in the second half of May and the first half of June. I guess that the supply of oakleaf caterpillars that all these birds rely on must have failed, because as I followed my route through the woods in the pouring rain I found box after box of dead baby birds, starved to death. That year only one pair in ten managed to successfully raise any young at all. And yet the following season, every single box was occupied as usual.

I put up a single box in my garden, on the fruit tree. It didn't seem worth putting one in the ash where the jackdaws almost always nested. The first year, it was occupied by a pair of great tits, bringing me back a splash of yellow just as the daffodils that filled the garden in March were starting to die back. But after that I decided to adapt the box, sawing a V-shaped notch beneath the entrance hole, and my plan to bring redstarts to the garden worked perfectly. They moved in the next spring and have remained ever since. Redstarts nest in crevices, in rocks as well as in tree holes, and my slight modification to the box was enough to make it more to their taste. While the garden wagtails bob and wag, the redstarts vibrate their long tails with a tremor so fast they are rendered almost invisible. I spent a good deal of time in the garden in the spring, digging the land, planting out the year's vegetables and weeding, and the redstarts became confident around me. While the female sat, the male came and perched on the wire, his beak filled with flying insects, showing off his black bib and bold white eyestripe, his slate-grey back, and his glorious robin-red breast and trembling tail.

The fields were full of lambs. The sheep invaded my dreams with their bleating and coughing. The lambs forever seemed to find themselves separated from their mother by a fence and bleated piteously while the ewe paced up and down the barrier that divided them, until finally I could take no more of it and went and shepherded the ewe the few yards to the open gate that would reunite them. And while I was out walking the fields it became second nature to liberate the occasional sheep that had trapped its head in a fence, again. They are not the brightest of creatures.

The months of April and May were busy times for the hill farmers. My farmer's nephew offered me a lift down to the village one spring day; there was a lamb on the passenger seat of his Land Rover that he was taking to the vet, so I picked it up and sat with it on my lap while it cried desperately. It had been born without a back passage, the farmer's nephew explained. Born without a back passage, and filling up fast. Every year my farmer had to hand-rear a handful of lambs, bottle-feeding them, perhaps one of a pair of twins born to a lame mother. When they saw him coming they bounded over, leaped into his arms and licked his face with excitement. The bond of affection between man and beast was beyond question. Yet the animals still all ended up in the same place, of course.

The butterflies that had slept the winter away in the corners of my ceilings upstairs had all woken now; one by one I let them out as I found them fluttering against my windows. The field mice were back to trying to raid my larder, but I was still awaiting the return of the bats to my loft. I had seen my first bats of the year though, not the long-eared bats but noctules, the largest species found in Britain. These bats are not house-dwellers, they live in tree holes, and I could recognize them by their different hunting style. They flew high and straight, purposefully searching out large flying insects such as moths, suddenly darting to one side to scoop up their prey, then returning to their original line as if they were following a predetermined route, as if they were running on rails.

One day I was drawn out into the garden, into the morning sunshine, by a peal of laughter. A green woodpecker, a male, was hopping about on the ground across the track, among the litter of stones that was once Penlan Farm. Green woodpeckers are less common here than the great spotted woodpecker, but in spring you wouldn't know it; the woods ring continually with their distinctive yelping laugh, far more a part of the soundtrack of spring than the drumming of their spotted cousins. The spotted woodpeckers rarely leave the trees, while the greens spend a lot of time on the ground searching for ants, something of a speciality of theirs. Once as a child I found the corpse of a long-dead green woodpecker. Only feathers and bone remained, the flesh had all gone save for its tough, wiry tongue. From its root in the bird's throat it divided into two and went backwards instead of forwards. The two strands travelled behind the dome of the bird's skull, then over the top of its head, rejoining between the bird's eyes and entering the beak. This incredible design meant that the bird would be able to protrude the barbed tip of its tongue to a distance longer than even its beak, perfect for exploring the tunnels of ants' nests, like the long tongue of an anteater. It is hard to conceive how such an extraordinary arrangement could have evolved, but there it was.

The woodpeckers seemed to be partial to this patch of hillside in front of my cottage. My assumption was that the rocks strewn around here, the rubble of the farmhouse, kept the soil drier than elsewhere and particularly suitable for ant nests. As I watched the male rootling around on the ground, I heard a call, and a female flew up the hill. Up and down, rising and falling, the characteristic undulating flight of a woodpecker. She perched on a bough of the ash tree nearest to the male, and he immediately flew up to join her. They were directly facing each other on opposite sides of an almost vertical branch, and kept craning their necks to peer at one another. Then the male slowly, slowly, unfolded his chequered wings until they formed a perfect fan. He held them open for a while, before just as slowly folding them. As soon as he was done, the female copied this move perfectly, then the male again, back and forth, back and forth. It was one of the most touching displays I have ever seen. And then, to an invisible cue, the two birds launched themselves simultaneously from their perch and flew off down the hill together, their lemony-yellow rumps bobbing side by side into the distance.

In the gnarly old ash just over the fence from my fruit tree there was a hole about fifteen or twenty feet up, a hole at least six inches across, too big to be suitable for small birds to nest in. This hole was perfectly situated for me to keep an eye on; it was visible from my front window, the window in the east wall that I watched my bird table from, my bedroom window, my porch, or when I was working in the garden. There was nothing special about this hole to make it stand out from a thousand others in the neighbourhood, but because of where it was located not much went on there that I missed. I don't mean only the birds that nested in it – it was actually not an ideal hole for most birds to nest in because it was not sunken at all, and its base was level with its entrance – but also any bird that even considered the possibilities it might have to offer.

The jackdaws visited this hole every year without exception, though they most often ended up choosing the tree on the rocks behind the house that I thought of as theirs. They always gave the chimneys a good inspection too. One February, I returned from a few days away to find the pair occupying my bedroom, roosting on top of the wardrobe. They must have come down the chimney exploring its potential and then found themselves unable to fly back up such a narrow chute. Judging from all the feathers left on my windowsill they had been desperately attempting to make their escape through my closed window, so it was lucky for them that I came back when I did.

A pair of stock doves came too without fail, shyly and diffidently inspecting the potential nesting site in the ash-tree hole. They seemed to spend a long time considering the matter, weighing up the pros and cons. It was strange how a bird that looked so similar to the town pigeon could have such a different disposition; these birds seemed quintessentially wild and wary. They provided another example of the precision of the rhythms that birds live by; they came for their visit each year just over a week after the curlews returned. I could predict their arrival in the ash to the day, or at most to within two days.

There was another annual visitor to the hole in the ash that was much more surprising; I could scarcely credit it when I first saw it. A snake-necked female goosander had come all the way up from the river. Goosanders are primitive-looking sawbill ducks that feed exclusively on fish, and seldom leave the water except to visit their tree-hole nests. They have very short legs and are obviously not designed for dry land. She would circle around and around my front fields, as if summoning up the courage, and then finally crash-land on to the tree, her wings flapping furiously, her feet scrabbling to gain a hold. She would spend many hours in my little clearing, carefully and methodically examining every tree in turn. She would even peer down my chimneys, and would sometimes decide this was a good spot for a break, perching a while immobile on the apex of my roof, like a straw bird on a thatch. When the goosanders' eggs hatch, the young must leave the nest almost immediately and follow their mother to the safety of the river. It is hard to contemplate the journey this would entail were the bird to nest all the way up on my hillside. What an incredible obstacle course this would be for the newborn ducklings.

But this year they were all too late; the nesting hole had been appropriated by the owls who last year used the dying oak fifty yards away at the nearest corner of Penlan Wood. Or rather, by last year's female, for this year she had a new mate: the pale grey male of last year had been usurped or had died. The female staked her claim incredibly early; just before New Year I saw her pay her first visit. It was dusk, and she had been calling relentlessly from within the dark depths of the wood. Then she flew over on silent wings to the ash and began to weigh up its possibilities, looking thoughtful, hesitant even. The whole time she kept on calling, a soft crooning call that I had not heard before and was audible only from close by. When the season came,

and she began to incubate, I was able to watch her as she sat
since the hole was not sunken, and as I worked in the garden I could see her eyes following me everywhere. And
when I looked up and could no longer see her I was able to
guess that the eggs had hatched. I donned my chainsaw
goggles for protection and shinned up the tree for a look.
The two tiny chicks must have been born that same day,
the eggshells were still in the nest, and the proud parents
had been busy collecting a buffet to welcome them, a pick-
and-mix of one long-tailed field mouse, one short-tailed
field vole, one bank vole and one pygmy shrew.

Because I knew the exact date of hatching, it was possible to arrange with the doctor at the field centre for the
young birds to be ringed at precisely the right stage in their
development. On the appointed day I scrambled back up
the tree to the hole. Although the nest was nearly twenty
feet up I didn't need a ladder; the old tree was so knobbly
and gnarly I could easily find footholds and handholds.
The young owls were now enormous balls of down that
looked disgruntled at being disturbed, and I put each one
in turn into a cloth bag and lowered it on a string to the
doctor waiting below. It would not be long before they
were ready to leave the nest. Soon they were jostling for
position at the entrance to their hole in order to be first
when the food arrived. The opening was not wide enough
for the two of them so inevitably they left the hole before
they were able to fly. First one and then the other scrambled up the tree trunk to the first available bough, and there
they perched, huddled side by side, blinking in the sunlight. They remained there for days, but eventually one

day I returned from a walk to find them missing from their branch. It didn't take long to locate them; they were calling for food from a tree about fifty yards away. I pictured them clambering down the tree trunk, then hopping and bounding across the hillside on their oversized feet, but in reality I had probably simply missed their first flight.

Spring was beginning to turn to summer, and the year's lambs were teenagers now, in sheep years. They hung around in gangs and used the path to my cottage as a race-track, thundering up and down it for hours each day. The woods were full to bursting with the year's fledglings, a bonanza for the hungry hawks. The brood of redstarts from my box had left the nest; as I walked around the garden they sprang unexpectedly from the ground at my feet and whirred away, until their clockwork apparently ran down and they slumped suddenly back to earth.

Early one morning I was out in my front garden when I saw the unmistakable slate-grey back of a male sparrow-hawk slipping low up the hillside straight towards me, right alongside the barbed-wire fence. He touched down momentarily on the rock just across the track – where the stoat had reared up and watched me that last winter gone – then with a single flick of his wings was on the fence post right before my eyes. I had never been so close to a sparrowhawk before, never imagined that I would be. His breast was delicately barred in pastel orange. His eyes were a piercing brilliant yellow, as were the clawed feet that clutched at the post convulsively. He was poised like a coiled spring, the intensity of his nervous tension was palpable.

He ruffled his feathers, he twitched, he jerked his head from left to right until he saw his mark, and then he struck. In the front field was a short row of tangled hawthorns and hazels, the last relic of a long-gone hedge, and he hurled himself into it. Claws snapped shut, and when he lifted off a moment later and sailed down towards the wood, a lifeless bundle trailed from the gibbet of his dangling talon. A second, luckier fledgling redstart flew panicking out of the same hawthorns and straight towards me, heading I suppose for the safety of its home box. It didn't quite make it; instead, it crashed into my leg and fell to the ground at my feet, cheeping piteously.

6. *The Bird in the Bush*

The goshawks caught me unawares. So far as I knew they had died out in Britain decades ago, and their stealthy return had passed me by completely. I don't know how many times I must have watched them unknowingly, but it was certainly months before I gave in to the evidence of my senses, for I was watching a creature that I believed to be extinct.

This is also a notoriously elusive bird to watch; even more so than the sparrowhawk it seems to live on the very periphery of human vision, and before you can turn to look at it, it has already gone. It is particularly hard to judge the size of a bird against an open sky because you have no frame of reference, and the goshawk is fundamentally an outsize sparrowhawk, with colouring and markings almost identical to those of the female of the smaller species. The male and female differ in size too, so the two species form a size gradient, from the little male sparrowhawk, barely bigger than a mistle thrush, to the big female goshawk, the size of a buzzard. In essence they are sparrowhawks writ large. Bigger, bolder, fiercer, faster. They have all the qualities I had learned to love in the sparrowhawk, but in overdrive.

I do remember the first time I allowed the merest thought of a goshawk to enter my mind, if only fleetingly.

It was during my first autumn at the cottage, and I was walking past the beech-hanger that clings on to the hillside halfway down towards the river. There had been a heavy crop of beech mast that year, and the woodpigeons had gathered for the feast. As I walked alongside the woodland edge, a bird of prey passed twenty feet over my head and into the wood, sending pigeons spouting out in all directions. Then it turned and crossed the valley ahead of me. It looked to be about the size of a buzzard, but something was not right; its tail was too long for one thing. As the bird settled into an isolated tree directly across the river from me, a dark cloud passed overhead and there was a sudden torrential shower of rain. I leaned into the broad grey trunk of the nearest beech for shelter, though I was dripping wet in seconds, and tried to keep my eye on the bird, but it was no use. Thick veils of rain gusted up the valley above the river and I could hardly make out the tree the bird had perched in, let alone the bird itself. A few minutes later, the rain stopped as suddenly as it had begun, and the sun came out, but the bird had slipped away. I quickly convinced myself that it had been a female sparrow-hawk and I had misjudged its distance and size. It seemed the only plausible explanation.

Over the course of that winter several of my sparrow-hawk sightings gave me pause for thought, but it was not until the following February that the evidence became incontrovertible. It was a dull, overcast day, one of those days when the birds seem to go into hiding, when even the ever-present buzzards stay in the trees listlessly, and it feels as though the whole world is still and poised, waiting for

the sun to shine again. In the field at the edge of the pine wood, on the hillside above my cottage, a flock of around twenty-five woodpigeons was feeding in the grass. This was about as large as pigeon flocks got here in the hills; you would never see the flocks of hundreds that you get in the lowlands on arable farmland. They all suddenly took to the air, in close formation and mounting fast, and I stopped dead in my tracks, for I knew that something exciting was about to happen. These birds had been spooked, and not by me; I was too far off.

I didn't have to wait long. A hawk burst over the top of the wood with quick, flicked-back wingbeats, and set off in pursuit of the fleeing pigeons. This rowing motion of the wings is distinctive, and immediately separates hawk from falcon, with even the briefest of glimpses. The flock was flying close and fast over the oak wood. Pigeons are no slouches on the wing themselves, but the hawk closed the gap in seconds. Right above them, it suddenly dropped. The cluster of pigeons momentarily spread out, then reformed. The hawk seemed to fall through a hole in the middle of them, and for a second it was surrounded by pigeons, all just out of reach, and then it was beneath them, empty-handed. It turned to resume the pursuit, but its one chance had been missed, and the element of surprise had been lost. It abandoned the chase, flew a single tight circle, and set off back over the wood. But there was no longer any denying it: this was a goshawk. It was too big to have been anything else.

I checked at the field centre and found that, yes, it was true, the goshawks had returned, and there was even a suspected nesting site a few miles down-valley. If the red kite had been brought back from the brink of extinction, the goshawk had long ago flown all the way over that brink and disappeared into the distance. While sparrowhawks are happy with our traditional rural landscape, the chequer-board of fields and hedgerows and copses that make up the vast bulk of our countryside, the goshawks need relatively large tracts of undisturbed woodland to live in. This was not a problem here as the valley was heavily wooded; in fact trees were the main source of revenue for the estate, more so than the rents of the tenant farmers. Long, long ago, when Britain was entirely covered with dense wood-land, the goshawks would have been numerous, the pole predator among the birds, but as the woods were hacked away over the centuries these birds were pushed back into the ever smaller and remoter pockets of remaining wood-land. And persecution finished them off. For decades there were no breeding records of goshawks in Britain. Perhaps a tiny handful clung on unnoticed; as I had found myself this was an incredibly easy bird to overlook. What is cer-tain is that their revival depended in part on birds that had escaped from falconers, or even been deliberately released, perhaps in combination with a few strays that had drifted over from the continent. The landscape they found was marginally more hospitable than it had been when their predecessors had died out; gamekeeping was in decline, the pesticides that threatened the future of so many of our birds of prey had been outlawed, and most importantly vast swathes of our uplands had been planted with huge tracts of conifer plantations. These alien forests of spruce may have caused a habitat loss that was hugely detrimental to many of our upland species, but for the goshawk they were a godsend.

As soon as I knew I had goshawks on the hill they became my holy grail, the bird I most hoped to see each new day as I woke. And I was amply rewarded. I saw them almost every day that spring. There was a pair of them, or at least there was a male and there was a female; I never once saw the two birds together. I kept a meticulous record of every sighting, savouring every moment, and formed a mental map of the flight path of each bird as I saw it, just as I had with the sparrowhawks when I first arrived here. Now that I had found these birds I wanted to understand them too, read the auspices, unlock the mystery hidden behind the turn of each bird's wing. The world I knew was a ball of wool, criss-crossed with a network of invisible pathways, like the gossamer that would be revealed only on a dewy morning. And I wanted to unravel it. If only the birds would leave contrails in the sky for me to follow, so that I would not always be left behind.

It was the time of year when my sparrowhawks became more active too, or at least more visible, beginning their spring display flights and staking their claim on Penlan Wood. That spring there was one gale after another, the westerly winds blew at fifty miles an hour, but still the hawks were out. Early one morning I was watching the birds on the bird table when the male cruised past just outside the window, sending the nuthatches and the tits dashing for cover. He was without intent; if he had been determined he would

not have been cruising. As he reached the front corner of the
cottage he was hit by the wind from the west, and for a few
moments the two opposing forces were equally matched, so
that the hawk hung motionless just two feet above the
ground. At this range and in this light the bird's upperparts
no longer looked a uniform slate grey, but were flecked with
gold. I could pick out every individual feather, the paler tip
of each one making the bird seem mottled, somehow more
complicated. He didn't need to fight back against the wind;
he looked about him, tilted his wings ever so slightly, and
slipped across and down the hillside until he was lost to view.

Later, a goshawk raced through the trees at the bottom
of the front field. He slalomed around the tree trunks at
waist height, using up every inch of cover. This was serious
hunting flight, and at the end of this hawk's trajectory an
unsuspecting bird was about to die, but the kill was out of
sight behind the corner of Penlan Wood. When I stepped
outside that day, the wind was so strong I could barely
stand upright. The goshawk had been flying directly into
that wind, at incredible speed, as if in defiance.

After so long being unable to see, or rather to recognize,
the goshawks, now I could hardly stop spotting them.
They were suddenly everywhere I went. It felt like an honour that they had chosen to share my very own patch of
hillside. A single crow diving wildly for cover alerted me
to a goshawk flying up from the valley bottom. He was flying at tree level, thirty or forty feet up, but the hillside was
steep, and he was having to work at it. With each flicker of
his wings he surged forward, and then slowed with each
soar. He passed close above the roof of the cottage, and I

rushed to the back door to see him off. As the hillside levelled off over the pine wood he began to pick up speed,
jerking to left and right and rolling as though tossed by
sudden gusts of wind. But now, now there was no wind.

That day the starlings returned and began to build their
nest in their favoured corner of my loft. One of them took
up its place on the topmost twig of the ash tree right in
front of the house, singing snatches of borrowed song.
Two days later it was there singing when it suddenly broke
off mid-phrase and threw itself down-valley as the black
shadow of the big female goshawk cruised above my roof
from behind. She effortlessly followed the twists and turns
of the desperate starling, but didn't pick up speed; this was
only a matter of habit for her. She had either already fed or
considered a starling too paltry a snack to trouble herself
over. A minute later, the starling was back on its perch,
preening itself silently. It looked decidedly ruffled.

Down the hill to collect my mail. A red kite swung over
the hilltop to join the circling buzzards and ravens. Birds of
prey so often seem to choose the same place at the same
time. The kite was joined by a partner, and the two floated
seemingly without effort over the hillside, then drifted
over the streamside woods. I followed them down, walking alongside the old cart track, churned up now by cattle,
and through the alder woods to the old bridge, where I
paused and sat on the crumbling stone wall for a while. A
goshawk careered over my head in search of pigeons. She
banked, she rocked, she turned, it was as if she were flying
through the trees rather than skimming their tops. She
twisted so fast that her long straight tail seemed almost to

lag behind her every move, as though if she went a little faster still she would have left it behind altogether. I barely had time to catch sight of the thick white eyestripe frowning like an eyebrow over a big, blood-orange eye. This was a fierce, swift, hungry bird, with killing on her mind. Down to the river, and there was the male bird, circling right above the water's edge in the company of four buzzards. He was barely smaller than them, and seemed to be trying to impersonate them. He soared in slow, lazy circles, opening and closing his long, heavily barred tail like a fan. But he could not help himself; compared to him the buzzards looked graceless and awkward. Twice he passed directly over me, rolling his head through ninety degrees, first to the left, then to the right, and looked down at me with his huge, fiery eye. I felt as though I was being pinned to the ground.

A circling hawk is a displaying hawk, and soon I would see the female's spring display flight too. Spring was truly here now, a clear blue sky dotted with only a few little white clouds. The first butterfly of the year, a peacock, flitted in through the open window and settled on my hand. I carried it out and went to check on the cluster of tortoiseshells that had slept the winter away in the corner of the upstairs ceiling. They were still hanging there, huddled together in suspended animation. A raven passed overhead, uttering a strangely delicate trill as if calling me, and I went outside to see. The raven pair was out too, circling over the hillside and flipping on to their backs in turn, showing off to one another, and a buzzard was soaring lazily and mewling, its broad motionless wings canted upwards. As they all drifted together against the clear blue sky, I saw another bird with them. One of the ravens made a single half-hearted pass at the slightly smaller female hawk, but she ignored it, rising above them. This was a big, powerful bird, barrel-chested like a falcon peregrine. She rose fast, turning in tight circles. Her back and tail were a dark brown, but on each turn the sunlight gleamed from her pale breast and most of all from the brilliant white feathers beneath her tail. She rose hundreds of feet, turned to the west, and briefly hung there immobile. Then she suddenly jerked back her wings and thrust herself forward. The acceleration was tremendous, like a jet plane during take-off, and instantly she was racing towards the open hills, a flicker of backswept wings, then a soar, then a flicker again, until she was nothing more than a black speck that winked out over the distant slopes of bracken.

It was not long before she was back. A pack of fifteen rooks, barefaced and baggy-trousered, were strutting around the back field. They suddenly all lifted into the air, alerting me to the arrival of a hawk – soaring then circling, masterful and elegant. She seemed to have no interest in the rooks, but the rooks were not prepared to let it go. A group of half a dozen split off and made for the trees of Penlan Wood, while the remainder, staying close together, gathered above the circling hawk and began to mob her, making a strange call that I hadn't heard before. One by one they dived the twenty feet that separated them from the hawk, though they took great care to veer away and up again when they were two or three feet above her. This was a serious business to them, no doubt, though to me it looked like nothing so much as a game of dare. And, in the end, the rooks won; the hawk tired of the game and was driven down into the valley.

With both the male and female starting to display, my hopes were raised that they might build their nest close to hand, and I began to speculate where might be most suitable. But it was not to be. My last sighting of a goshawk that spring was at the very beginning of April. I was down at the well replenishing my water supply, and when I turned back towards home I could see a whirl of wings racing around my cottage. It was two buzzards and a goshawk, racing in tight, fast circles around the cottage at chimney height. It was impossible to say who was chasing whom; they were equidistant from one another. I had never seen a buzzard moving so quickly, and I could hardly believe they had it in them. Then the hawk suddenly shot vertically upwards, doubling its height in a moment. I don't know how it did it; it seemed like a physical impossibility. It folded its wings and stooped, jackknifing into one of the buzzards at a forty-five-degree angle. The hapless buzzard was knocked sideways by the blow and fell to the ground like a stone, the hawk with it, carried to the ground with the impetus of its own blow. The second buzzard swung into action, and the hawk raced off along the top of Penlan Wood. The stunned bird stood there motionless just over my garden fence, its wings splayed like a drying cormorant's, its beak wide and its tongue lolling. This had been the work of the smaller male goshawk; had it been the larger female I doubt the buzzard would have ever got up again.

★

The goshawks disappeared from my landscape as suddenly as the male had struck down this buzzard. I watched out for them constantly, scanning my horizons, my focus drawn by every distant crow or pigeon, but in my heart I knew that they were gone; their absence was almost tangible. All summer long, while the other birds of prey were at their most visible and active, I had no sightings at all on my hill. And then, come September, they were back, as if they had just been on a summer break. And this became the pattern; in autumn, winter and spring I had goshawks; in summer I had none. Though I never again had such a concentration of sightings as that spring when I first found them. There was a rationale for this seasonal absence: in the breeding season they needed to stay in close proximity to the nest, and they could afford to as their prey was at its most plentiful. So in summer their range contracted, just as mine was expanding.

I can probably visualize every goshawk sighting I have ever had; each seems unique and unforgettable. My most recent sighting was in almost exactly the same place as my first definite sighting long ago. She flew out towards me from the edge of my pine wood, slow and stately. A massive, powerful bird, how could I ever have mistaken her for a sparrowhawk? She flew lazily and inattentively, and saw me long after I had first spotted her. She was almost on top of me when she finally noticed me; she pulled up sharp, wheeled around and flew away in the direction she had come from. I followed the invisible pathway right to the spot where she had emerged from the wood. Inside the fenced area was a freshly killed rabbit. I had not missed the kill by long; the blood was still flowing, seeping into the grass. The goshawk had eaten nearly half of it, and I wondered whether she planned to return for the rest later or would abandon it now she'd had her fill. This wood harbours more rabbits than anywhere else on this side of the river. They dig their burrows all around the fringes of the wood, and emerge to feed in the fields alongside. They are timid though; they stay close to the edge of the wood, and race for cover at the slightest disturbance. Perhaps this rabbit had thought it was home and dry when it had made it through the fence; its corpse still pointed inwards, towards its burrow, towards safety.

I walked slowly around the perimeter of the wood, though I knew I would not see the hawk again now; she would be far away from here, resting off her meal in the dark heart of a different wood. At the far edge, almost directly opposite, I found the remains of a second rabbit, perhaps a couple of days dead, its plucked fur sifting through the trees. I wondered if one day the hawks might choose to summer here, and make this wood their own. This plantation is growing up fast, the trunks are stout columns now and it is gathering that monumental solemnity of the mature wood of Scots pine. There are broad rides through the trees that I carved with my own chainsaw, runways down the hill for the racing hawk. And of course it is stuffed with rabbits. The truth is, this wood will probably never be big enough for goshawks, but you can always hope.

The goshawks should have been the most frustrating of birds; they would disappear for long periods without warning and they would often tantalize with fleeting appearances, which were often not even enough to offer me a definitive identification, and yet I prized these sightings almost more than those of any other bird. Perhaps the challenges were part of the reward; perhaps this is why some people will go to such great lengths to pursue rarities. Of course if I wanted a good look at a goshawk I could easily have gone to a falconry centre and stared at one all day, eyeball to eyeball; I could even have flown one myself if I had taken a little trouble to organize it. I am sure that would have been a worthwhile experience, but in some respects it would not have been the same thing at all. The bird in the bush is worth ten in the hand. We take pleasure from watching birds partly because they are beautiful, but the birds that we see in our minds are more than just feather and bone, their appeal is not simply aesthetic. We watch them because of what they tell us about ourselves, and about our sense of what it means to be wild and free.

7. *The Thief*

There was a ritual I performed late every spring, whenever I felt that the time had come. I would take my bow saw off its hook on the woodshed wall and stroll down the hill to the stream. There I would work my way through the streamside hazels in search of the perfect hazel wand, just the right weight and thickness. I would take my time; the staff I would cut would be my companion all summer long. My summer season was a long one; when it was still spring in the woods, when the birds were still busy singing and nesting, I considered it summer in the hills. And when the leaves and the mushrooms were telling me that autumn had long since come, I would still be holding on. So long as there was life on the moors, and the weather was good enough to walk them, it was still my mountain summer.

As I wandered around the fields close to my home, I would often run into the farmer, and he would occasionally ask me to lend him a hand with whatever he was doing, if I wasn't too busy. Which, let's face it, I seldom was. Perhaps he would ask me to hold a reel of barbed wire while he restrung a fence. Or perhaps I would get sheepdog duties, guarding an open gate to make sure the sheep being rounded up didn't make their escape. The farmer had two sheepdogs, a dog and a bitch, but the dog he described as the worst sheepdog in the world, and it was handy to have me there in case the dog noticed a squirrel, or had an itch that needed scratching, or felt like a quick nap. While I kept the farmer company, he would talk to me a little, mostly about sheep farming. He would pause and put his hand to his head and tip back his cap so that its peak pointed to the sky, and tell me stories about foot-rot and twins, about gelds and thieves. A geld is a ewe that has failed to produce a lamb, while a thief is one of the year's lambs that has escaped the trip to market, and has instead been put up on the open sheepwalk to roam free for a season. A thief of time.

I too was a thief; I had stolen myself away from the world and had the freedom of the hills, for now at least. When I set off for the moors, often the steepest climb of the day would be my back field. The mountains here are whale-backed, smoothed by time. The sides are steep, but I was already high up on the hillside; once I was on the tops there were hundreds of square miles of rolling moorland, uninhabited and unfenced. The further I walked the wilder the land became, as the number of grazing sheep that had made it this far began to reduce. There were half-wild ponies up here too, with long shaggy manes. They would not run off but nor would they approach; instead they would freeze when they saw me and stare right back at me through their fringes for as long as I was in view. When the weather allowed, I would pack a bag, take my trusty staff, and set off on a sunny morning, not to return home for two or three or four days. I would walk into the westerly wind, with the clouds scudding towards me, making the hills a patchwork of light and shadow. The weather changed so quickly up here, but I could see for miles, and sometimes I would see the showers coming an hour before they reached me. This was a land of rainbows.

All day long I roamed the tops, then as the afternoon began to wear on I would walk to the first stream I came to and begin to follow it down. I would stop at the head of the valley, as soon as there was the first scattering of rowans and hawthorns, enough fallen sticks for me to build a small fire. Then I would find a dry, level patch of clear ground alongside the stream, light my fire, and boil up water in an old tin can with the lid folded back as a handle. I would make myself tea and eat whatever I had brought with me, and as darkness fell I would climb into my sleeping bag, lie back and look at the stars. I had the tiniest one-man tent too, only a few pounds in weight, as a contingency for a sudden change in the weather.

It is hard to do justice to the beauty of the night sky in these hills. With no light pollution for miles around, the gaps between the stars seemed to shrink to nothing. If I focused on the space between any two stars, more stars would appear to fill that space, and then still more to fill the spaces between them. The night sky became not a sprinkling of stars against a black backdrop, but a wash of unbroken light. The Milky Way was no longer milky; it had curdled, solidified like scrambled eggs in a pan. I would step outside on a clear night and it would make me gasp. I could never get used to it. And deep in the summer, when the Perseids came, there would be shooting stars every few seconds all night long. Drifting through space since time immemorial, then suddenly burning up in a blaze of glory, witnessed by no one save for me, by sheer chance looking at the right spot in the sky at the perfect moment. One night, sitting by my little fire by a mountainside stream counting off the shooting stars, I noticed a spectral green glow in the bracken beside me and followed the light to its source. A glow-worm, the first I had ever seen here, shining in the night like a star that had come to earth.

Some of the places I found to camp in were magical, rock-strewn cirques cut off from the world below by deep plantations of spruce, enclosed and sheltered from the wind like an amphitheatre. A tumbling waterfall with a pool to bathe in. The white rumps of the wheatears darting from rock to rock. At dusk the piping of the ring ouzel, the rare mountain blackbird, and sometimes a glimpse of them feeding in the rowans. The bracken buzzing with whinchats. I found the whinchats a mystery: one valley would be full of them, the next empty. I never saw them down in the lower valleys, except at one single location on my lanes, where they nested in the hedge every year. I watched them here many times, asking myself what made this particular length of hedgerow, this particular field, different from all the others, and never finding an answer. On my nights out in the hills, I would wake chilled in the early dawn, and relight my fire to warm myself before I packed and set off for the tops again. I remember one morning waking to see a young vixen prancing through the long grass towards me, meadow pipits fluttering around her head like a cloud of flies. She was far from home, having probably spent the night searching for eggs. There were so many pipits nesting up here that I regularly stumbled on their nests. The vixen spotted me and paused in her tracks, front leg cocked like a pointer. She had probably never seen a human before and didn't know quite what to make of me. I reached into my pack, found a biscuit and held it out towards her; she came a little closer before retreating, then started to close in again. This approach and retreat continued for a minute or two, with her gaining just a little ground each time. I don't know if she would have eventually fed from my hand; I thought better of giving her the wrong idea about people and tossed the biscuit over to her. She flinched as I threw, then came and grabbed the biscuit and trotted off with it held proudly in her jaws.

Sometimes you can walk these hills for hours at a time without seeing very much at all. On these open expanses silence prevails, and they can seem empty, devoid of life. But any longueurs would suddenly be interrupted by moments when a whole host of birds would appear at once: a peregrine dashing over the crags, a hovering kestrel, a pair of soaring kites, a displaying curlew or jinking snipe. Many of our true upland species are rare and spread thinly over huge areas of seemingly featureless moor. The merlin for instance – the moorland falcon – has a population of perhaps only around a hundred pairs in the whole of Wales, so looking for them was like diving for pearls.

My first sighting of a merlin in these moors has never been equalled. I was deep in the hills, more than a day's walk from home, and was following the ridge line west. There is a long stretch of concrete marker posts over the mountains, and from each one you can just about make out the next, so they make a useful waymarker across these vast open spaces. I believe they show the limit of the catchment area for the reservoirs many miles below. I was approaching one when a merlin slipped low across the hillside towards me and alighted on the post, ruffling up its feathers as it landed. It was a little male, barely bigger than a thrush, and sat only a few feet away. He was subtly coloured in delicate pastel reds and blues, except for his brilliant yellow legs with jet-black talons that made it look like he had been painting his nails. His minuscule hooked beak made me think of a parakeet or a budgerigar rather than a bird of prey. I had frozen, and he seemed quite unconcerned by my proximity. We waited like this, both still and alert, until finally he took off. He soared in a low arc just above the ground, and disappeared into a nearby bank of heather about fifty yards away. It seemed that I had found not only a merlin, but also a merlin's nest, though I didn't follow him to inspect the site, and I never found the territory again, even with the long line of posts to guide me. All that summer I watched out for merlins, in the hope of seeing them once more, but they eluded me until the very end of the season when I had given up hope of seeing another that year. It was to be my last overnight walk that summer; the weather was getting ready to turn. I was far from my previous sighting, having headed out to see the biggest waterfall in reach of the cottage, perhaps ten or fifteen miles out. At dusk, as I was preparing to camp beside the tumbling waters, a wheatear came hurtling down the steep hillside right alongside the falling stream, twisting and swerving and looping through the gorse bushes, with a female merlin right on its tail, just an inch or two behind it.

Once, early in the season, I was returning from one of my overnight expeditions when the clouds fell, a thick fog descended, and I became well and truly lost for the first and only time. I climbed to a mountaintop cairn to see if it would lift me above the clouds so that I could regain my sense of direction, but it was no use, I could see no further than ten or twenty yards. I looked at the cairn more closely; I had been here earlier, I had just spent an hour walking in a circle. I wasn't too worried, for I knew that if I walked to the first stream I came to and then followed it down, it would eventually lead me off the hills, and even if I ended up many miles from home I would be able to get a lift back. It was still fairly early in the day, so there was no risk of being stuck here overnight with no remaining food. So I shrugged my shoulders and headed down in a random direction.

When I had come down off the steep side of the mountain I found myself in the most incredible blasted landscape that I had ever seen up here: a rolling sea of sticky black peat, studded with thousands of tiny heather-capped islands. The sides of these hummocks were often vertical or even overhanging, so I had to leap from one to the next over the deep runnels between them, or sometimes clamber down and wade ankle-deep through the bog if the gap was too wide. The landscape, lost in fog, looked primeval. I sat down for a while to soak up the atmosphere. A pair of red grouse burst from the heather beside me and clattered away, coughing like old men. Red grouse are a rarity on these moors; they feed almost entirely on young heather and there is very little heather on these hills because they are so heavily grazed. But not so many of the sheep that roamed this moorland in the summer made it out this far, and those that did would have been largely confounded by the steep sides of these mounds of peat. And then I heard it: a spectral wail that echoed through the fog like nothing I had ever heard before. This was the sound of broken hearts, a sound that could make the mountains weep. He emerged through the drifting fog, a golden plover already in his summer plumage, crisp black and white in front, spangled with gold on his back. He stood aloft a little hillock of heather only a few yards away, threw back his head and called to the skies. And then his answer came, again and again. There was a plover on every mound that was near enough for me to see through the fog; I could make out six of them in all, in a perfect circle around me, all facing inward, all calling. I don't know how long this carried on for – time had stood still – but then they were suddenly gone; they didn't fly, they just strode off into the fog and faded away. As I started to breathe again, there was a fleeting parting of the clouds and I was able to make out a few distant hills and work out exactly which way I should head for home.

This peatbog I had chanced upon was within daily reach of my cottage, and became a favourite destination. It was the closest thing to wilderness I had. These hills may have looked remote and untouched, but in fact they were shaped by the hand of man, and more specifically by man with sheep. If grazing were to stop, the grass would first be overtaken by heather, and eventually all but the highest peaks would be blanketed with sessile oak woods as they once had been. Even in this desolate bogland I found a few thick stumps of ancient oak emerging from the black mud, perhaps many thousands of years old. But it was isolated, bleak, and alien in its beauty, and it drew me back again and again. It was like taking a trip to another world.

On the first warm, sunny day after that first visit, I returned in the hope of seeing the plovers again. It was a fine walk of about three hours each way. I took my trusty staff and set off slowly up the back field, pausing occasionally, not wanting to tire myself before I had begun. Where the hillside levelled was the last gate on to the moor, the last gate in twenty miles. I didn't need to cross the summit of my hill, rather I followed the drystone wall where the highest fields joined the moor. A sparrowhawk was cruising the line too, relaxed in the sunshine. A swallow flew up from the fields below, where it had been scooping up insects hovering above the grass. It began to swoop in graceful arcs around the hawk, then was joined by another and another, until finally the hawk was trailing a retinue of perhaps a hundred of them in a whirling, darting cloud. They were drawn to the hawk like iron filings to a magnet.

My hill was a spur of the mountains, joined by a boggy saddle to a much bigger black hill that stretched miles to the west. I didn't often cross the top of this mountain. For one thing, it was covered with thick tussocks of moor grass that were extremely hard to walk through; in fact, local people refer to this grass as disco grass, because of the strange contortions you have to go through as you make your way across it. Also, the vast open expanses that topped this mountain were tilted southwards, so while they afforded great views many miles to the south, I would not be able to see the mountains to the west and north where I was headed until I was halfway there. It is good to be able to see your destination getting steadily nearer as you walk. This hill was fine for a short cut home, but for now I made a diagonal crossing of the boggy ground that was the source of my stream, and headed for the northern slopes of the black hill. Here it was quite different from the open top; the sheepwalk was close-cropped turf amid a scree of rocks where the wheatears bounced, and though it was very steep to walk across there were sheep trails to follow. Sheep trails are not reliable; they diverge, converge, fade away to nothing, but the sheep were at least good at picking the safest way to cross the frequent rain gulleys that dissected the mountainside. There was a fine view down to the sheltered valley below. The bottom end of the valley, to the north of my own hill, was forested with oak below the slopes of head-high bracken. This was beautiful mature woodland, in the midst of which raced a stream hidden in a deep dingle, a succession of cascades and pools. The upper reaches of the valley were the most marginal of marginal land; fields that had never been drained or improved, where the hares played. The whole valley was dotted with the ruins of abandoned farmsteads, the ruins outnumbering the handful of occupied dwellings.

As I picked my way across one of the dry gullies, I put up a kestrel from the hillside below me, and he flew across the valley to join his mate hovering opposite, making use of the thermals that rose up the mountainside, as was a solitary soaring kite. As I watched them, the female dropped three times in quick succession, snatching up dung beetles, I assumed. A peregrine came sailing into view over the hilltops, and the kestrels immediately stopped their hovering and ascended fast to rise above the intruder. They knew that it wouldn't be safe to stay low. The peregrine circled lazily above me, taking a break from her eyrie, her wings outspread, her tail slightly fanned, and gave me a fine view of her hooded head. And above her circled the two kestrels, one of which repeatedly made fleeting swoops at the much bigger peregrine, taking great care not to drop below her. The peregrine for the most part ignored the attention, until at last the kestrel's pestering got a little too bold and she flipped on to her back and presented her claws.

She began to circle more determinedly, rising fast in a true hunting flight, with the kestrels struggling to stay above her. They seemed tiny in comparison to her, like wasps buzzing about her head. Eventually she rose so high above the valley that she was herself no more than a speck, while the kestrels had disappeared from view altogether. When she finally drifted down, one of the kestrels had slipped away, but the other was still hanging above her, still bothering her, and she finally tired of these attentions and began to chase the kestrel across the valley, mirroring its every move like a merlin pursuing a pipit. She peeled away and resumed her leisurely circling, unmolested now that the kestrel had hotfooted it across the valley, but there was no prey for her here. She folded her wings and began to slip downwards, at first slowly and then with gathering speed. For a brief moment I thought she was about to stoop on some unseen victim, but then she levelled off and raced for the hills, an anchor in the sky.

At the head of the valley, a vast glacial sweep links these hills to the mountains opposite, wild and featureless save for a scattering of collapsed cairns and a lone standing stone, their significance lost in time. As I picked my way slowly across this bare expanse, a curlew suddenly flushed from close by and began to circle above me, calling in alarm, and its mate flew up from further off and joined it. Wader nests are notoriously hard to find, and the curlew would not have flushed from the nest but would have crept some distance away before rising. But there it was, right at my feet, the merest scrape in the earth among the tufts of grass, four mottled eggs beautifully camouflaged. I attempted to triangulate the spot using the nearby peaks for reference, but I knew I would never find this nest again, the ridge was so huge and bare and open, the exact location so indistinguishable from any other.

The end of the ridge was marked by a solitary boulder, abandoned there long ago I supposed by the retreating glacier, and I paused there and looked back before I began the ascent of the winding path up the mountainside. The curlews had settled back on to their nest and ceased their constant calling. On this mountainside was a single steep ravine, and in that ravine was an isolated rowan, a mountain ash, far, far above any other trees. And in that rowan was a crows' nest. The pair of carrion crows that nested here had faced a challenge: how to build a nest in a place where there were no sticks. The nest was constructed entirely out of the bones of sheep.

The track that cut across the face of the mountainside was probably only used a few times a year, for rounding up sheep on horseback, or in a very, very carefully driven Land Rover. Where the track levelled off and switched back, we parted company, and I set off across the roughest of rough ground into a boggy, rush-filled hollow, where snipe jinked away as I picked my way through. One more climb, steep but short, and I was looking out over the peat-hag. With no fog to obscure the view, I could see the extent of the place for the first time; it reached as far as the eye could see, as if it was a whole barren world unto itself. The view shrank as I stepped down into it. It was like entering a maze, the heather-capped hillocks between which the soggy black runnels twisted and turned were hedge high, and I knew there would be no chance of identifying the place where I had found the plovers. I listened out for them instead, but this was a still, silent place, and even the pipits and larks were hushed. In the midst of the bog was a low, grassy ridge, and as I rounded this I came upon a hidden tarn. A little female teal, a mountain duck, saw me and quickly led her brood of ducklings into the cover of the rushes that fringed one side of the tarn. On the thick mat of brilliant green sphagnum moss that lined my side of the pool was a toad. It seemed unlikely that toads would breed here; unlike frogs, which will spawn in any available pond, toads are loyal to their traditional breeding grounds, and will travel considerable distances to get to them. At the nearest breeding lake that I knew of, the toads gathered in the spring in vast numbers, and the nearby roads had toad-crossing signs to try to keep the number of casualties down.

But that lake was at least fifteen miles away. I had been surprised enough to find a toad taking up residence under the
brick pedestal beneath one of my water-butts, but to find
one of these sedate, slow-moving creatures so far out in the
hills seemed extraordinary.

It was a hot, sunny day, and the walk had been arduous,
so I decided to see if the tarn was deep enough for swimming. The water was icy cold, and the lake bed was soft and
spongy apart from a few scattered boulders. It had been
impossible to see the bottom through the peat-tinged water
but it was just deep enough for a swim, and it was like bathing in red wine. After I had dried myself in the sunshine, I
took a circuit of the lake. As I picked my way through the
peat at the far side, there was a single call of alarm from
right by my feet, and a bird ran off, then stopped, then ran
again, trailing a convincingly broken wing. A classic distraction display that could mean only one thing – that a
plovers' nest was not far away. It was four eggs in a little
scrape; just like the curlews' only smaller. It was a beautiful
site, in miniature, at the very tip of a little grassy promon-
tory that protruded far out into the black sea. Having
established that golden plovers were nesting here and that I
had not simply stumbled on a party lost in the fog, I called
it a day and set off back to Penlan. As I crossed the glacial
ridge on my way home, the curlews were in the air and calling repeatedly, locked in battle with the crows from the nest
of bones.

Back home on the hill, this was a time of visitors, of trips
out with friends to places I would never otherwise see; to

far hills and lakes, and to the coast. A time of making use of people's transport to stock up with cans and bottles in preparation for leaner days to come. A time of cooking outside, of long summer evenings sitting out as the sun set and the bats began to emerge from under the gables. My garden, all yellows in spring, was a riot of pinks and purples from the mallows and foxgloves that were in full bloom. The summer silence was beginning to fall as the chorus of birdsong was snuffed out, one species at a time. Eventually, only the last chiffchaffs were calling in the woods, and the last yellowhammers on the hill, and then they lapsed into silence too. In June, the woods had been hectic with birds hunting food for their young, and in July there had been newly fledged young birds everywhere earning their wings, but as summer began to peak, the birds vanished into the depths of their annual moult. Even birds that were a constant presence in the spring, such as the pied flycatchers, seemed to disappear into thin air. August is notoriously the quietest month of the year for birdwatching; it is perhaps ironic that in the weeks when most people have the chance to get out into the countryside, there is less to be seen than at any other time of the year. Fortunately the birds of prey came into their own on these late-summer days; with the exception of my missing goshawks they seemed more active, more visible than ever. In part it was the dearth of most other birds that brought them to the fore, that made their presence more conspicuous, and in part it was that, as their prey hid itself away, they had to spend more and more time out hunting.

Some birds of prey tend to breed late. Like all birds they

try to make the period when they have a nest filled with hungry mouths to feed coincide with the time when food is most plentiful. While for the ravens this meant breeding early to catch the lambing season, for the sparrowhawks this meant waiting for the bonanza of newly fledged birds in the early summer. As the summer wore on and so many birds disappeared into the thickets for the moult, the hawks struggled to find enough food for their young, pushing the young hawks to leave the nest. By August, overcrowding and the young birds' impatience to be the first to be fed had led to them all abandoning their home. They hadn't gone far though; they still weren't ready to hunt for themselves and would wait in the woods in the vicinity of the nest, calling their hunger, over and over. I would listen out for them; the call was instantly recognizable once you knew it, the sound of an oversized squeaky toy. One August I found three new nesting sites by tracking down the relentless squealing coming from deep within a wood. The young birds would be scattered among the trees surrounding the nest, hunched up and cross-looking, all trying to ignore one another. Near by would be the plucking post, a drift of feathers around a tree stump that was the hawks' midden and would show you precisely what the birds had been catching and killing.

It was time for a final trip to the quarry, to try to catch sight of the peregrines one last time before they abandoned the hills for the winter season, so I set off over the ridge on a short cut to the north. I was barely halfway there when I surprised the tiercel from a trackside oak. He alighted from the tree and circled above me, winnowing his wings and screaming beautifully, and I wondered if this sighting meant that they had already left the eyrie. When I finally reached the quarry, a light drizzle had begun, and I was even less hopeful. But there was the falcon, soaring in the rain in front of the high crags, racing after a passing swift. Right behind her was her youngster, just the one, working hard to copy her every move. The two birds began to make false passes at one another, then little dummy stoops. It was a flying lesson.

On my way back, the drizzle stopped and the sun came out, so I took a break by the riverside, north of my usual beat. There was a long sweeping bend in the river here, and the water ran slow and deep. Dragonflies hovered over the stands of rushes and yellow flags that fringed the opposite bank, and on the grassy slope that led down to the water bounded a mink, a dark chocolate-brown female, spiky from the wet, which looked like a cross between an otter and a stoat. Normally when I saw them they were in the process of disappearing from view, but not this one; she scampered back and forth, back and forth, as if she were looking for something she had lost.

Leaning from the bank at the furthest reach of the river's curve was a dead tree, and on a branch of it that overhung the slow-moving water was perched a falcon, a hobby, my first here. It had the crimson thighs and rump of an adult, but not the black chevrons on white that make the adult bird look almost like a miniature peregrine. Instead of white, its breast was the russet of an autumn leaf. This bird's plumage was midway between that of a juvenile and

an adult; it was a wandering first-year bird that had roamed
far north of its usual haunt. Soon it would have to turn its
face back to the south, for these are migratory falcons and
it would have an unguided journey to Africa ahead of it. It
slipped off its branch and darted low across the water
towards me. Over the bankside rushes its talons snapped at
a dragonfly like it was plucking a flower. It ate the insect in
flight as it circled around and flew back to its perch, but not
before it had snipped off the wings and discarded them.
The diaphanous wings of the dragonfly floated down to
the water below and drifted slowly past me. The hobby
flew again and again, and never missed; it would take a lot
of these insects to satisfy its hunger. But eventually it was
found on its perch by a pair of magpies, and they began to
mob it so relentlessly, so unceasingly, that it admitted
defeat and flew on round the river's bend, and was lost to
view.

8. *The Still Point*

Moving water has its own magnetism. It always drew me back; I must have visited the river at least twice a week, in every season, in every weather. Some of the creatures I saw there I would never see anywhere else. A solitary female goosander may have had a bizarre annual excursion to my rooftop, but other than that I would only see them on the river: either swimming, or resting on a boulder midstream, or flying directly above the water. I don't recall ever having seen one on the riverbank. Not only did the river have its own distinct set of resident species, but it also had its own summer and winter visitors. It had its own array of passage migrants too, such as the goldeneye, or the osprey – just occasionally, tantalizingly glimpsed as they passed through – which had neither their breeding grounds nor their wintering grounds here, but used the river as a highway between the two. I never knew quite what to expect when I went to the river.

What happened beneath the surface was a mystery to me. I knew there were salmon and trout here, though this was no longer the fishing river it once had been. And I knew there were pike here too, because I could sometimes make out a monster lurking at the edge of a deep pool by the bridge. But I had no idea what other coarse fish there were, or what the fish that rose for floating insects and left fading ripples in their wake were, or what the huge shoals of tiny fry that scattered from the shallows in the summer when I waded in to bathe were. And I had no one who could fill this gap in my knowledge. I was no fisherman; my only experience of fishing was a short spell on a commercial fishing boat in the Baltic, and what I had learned there was not going to help me here. I could see the attraction of spending long days at the river's edge, away from it all, my attention fully focused, but I didn't feel I needed to justify this with a rod and line.

The river here was totally different in character from the reedy, winding, slow-moving rivers of the lowlands. The steep banks were heavily wooded. Where the river bent, beaches and islands of discs of pale grey shale gathered and built on the inside of the bend, and here alders tried to get a foothold in the shifting stones. Where the river narrowed, and in its shallower reaches, the water raced and tumbled over the boulders in miniature rapids. There might be quieter stretches too, where the clear water ran slow and deep beneath the overhanging trees, and all seemed calm and placid, but this could change dramatically. A sudden spate could see the water levels rise five or ten feet overnight. And occasionally the river would burst its banks, and the flood pools in the riverside fields would fill with dabbling mallards escaping the chaos of the river. After a storm or a sudden thaw I would go down to the footbridge and watch the roiling waters below, the colour of a pale lemon tea yesterday but a frothy cappuccino today, seething and churning down the valley, carrying everything with them. This bridge was suspended high above the water, and it needed to be, for the force of the storm water could wrench full-grown trees from the banks and send them sailing seaward, at least until the waters abated and they snagged somewhere downriver.

I'm not sure quite what it is with river birds and bobbing. The grey wagtails – grey on their backs only, their breasts being a beautiful citrus yellow – would be wagging their tails relentlessly as they scampered along the shale beaches; and the sandpipers would race low above the surface of the water, their wings stiff and hooded like a miniature umbrella, making their piercing triple calls, and then would alight on a midstream rock and begin to teeter, bouncing as if their knees were spring-loaded, as if they were trying to keep time with the dipper bobbing on a rock near by. Perhaps living in this watery light, this world in constant motion, made them this way. Maybe by matching their movements to the roll of the waters they were camouflaging themselves, making themselves invisible to predators above, or prey below. To my eyes, their restlessness – especially that of the wagtails and sandpipers, whose backs were the precise colour of shale – rendered them far more visible than if they remained still for a moment. But to a hawk soaring above, maybe a still point in a shifting world would be more likely to draw its hunter's eye.

The sandpipers were migrants, and many of the wagtails would move to lower ground in the hard weather too, but the dippers were always there – the totem bird of these fast-moving waters. If you were first to see one isolated from its environment you wouldn't think it a bird of the water at all; they are stumpy birds, reminiscent of an outsize robin, though a rich chestnut and mahogany, and with a white bib instead of an orange one. But *in situ* they could not look more at home, as they bob on the rocks by the rapids and dive repeatedly into the water to feed from the river-bed. I once took advantage of being with a friend who had a watch to time a dipper that was busily feeding. In half an hour it dived just over a hundred times, more than three times a minute. Not only was it catching invertebrate prey, such as caddis-fly larvae, but it was also regularly hopping out of the water with small fish in its beak, which it would then beat on its rock before swallowing whole. They had the river divided up between them and where territories met there would be constant skirmishes. I listened out for when they began to sing each year, and without fail they would begin just before New Year's Day. It would have been optimistic to think of it as an early sign of spring, but it lifted the heart nonetheless.

They were among the very first birds to nest, building in February and sitting before the end of March. I could see the reasons why the ravens nested early, even the long-tailed tits, but with the dippers I had no clue, and I could only assume it was something to do with the inscrutable life cycles of their underwater prey. At least they built dome nests, like the tits, that would help protect eggs and young from frosts. The dippers liked their nests to be directly over the water; their favourite sites, occupied year after year, were under the bridges, or rather culverts, where streams met the river, but there were not quite enough of these to go round. One winter I was able to watch from the footbridge as the resident pair collected moss and began to build their nest at the very tip of an overhanging beech bough that stretched far out across the river. They completed the nest and had begun to line it, but I could see that they had made an error of judgement: the nest was only about five feet or so above the water's surface, and the thaw in the mountains had not yet come. A few days later when I returned, the nest was underwater, and when the waters fell, the nest had been washed away. They were determined, though; as soon as the flood waters had abated, they started over in exactly the same place.

The stream came racing down the bank and into the river over ten or fifteen yards of bare rock, not quite steeply enough to be a waterfall. Wading into the culvert was like entering a tunnel, or a cave. It was a concrete pipe about three yards across and ten yards long, perfectly round save for a ledge halfway up both sides that stretched for its full length. Midway along this ledge were the dipper nests. There were four or five on each side, the newly built one a still-green mossy football, the older ones faded brown and progressively more and more disintegrated. On the remains of one of the old nests the wagtails had built a home of their own. As I reached the new nest I slipped my fingers in through the entrance hole to feel if laying had begun, and as I did so something dark and massive came hurtling through the tunnel towards me. In the confined space its head seemed as broad as a shovel, its whiskers like the bristles of a broom, and its tail as thick as my arm. Its back rippled and rolled,

as if a wave ran through it. It splashed through the water
by me, just a foot away, then slithered down the rocks to
disappear into the river. A dog otter, far bigger than any
of those I had seen in Scotland. I don't know what induced
this animal to run towards me rather than away from me;
if it had turned and slipped upstream I would probably
never have seen it, much as I will undoubtedly have
missed other otters that have seen or heard or scented me
first. I can only assume that we had surprised each other
equally, at exactly the same moment, and it had to get
past me to reach the ultimate safety of the deep water that
lay beyond me.

   This was a different experience to seeing otters on an
island beach in Scotland; river otters are supremely secretive, and their territories cover a huge range. The habitat
here was certainly right for them, and the population of
my river was probably as good as anywhere. If there was a
protracted dry spell in the summer I would always head
down to my nearest stretch of the river. This was a perfect
territory for otters, very secluded and heavily wooded on
both banks. On my side of the river the bank was vertical
for the first eight or ten feet, and it was only when the
water levels were at their very lowest that I could get below
this. The shrunken river at this time would expose little
coves of grey sand, a highway for anything making its way
along the riverside. Without fail I would find otter prints
in every stretch of sand, rounded pads compared to the
more spidery trail of the mink. In fact, there would always
be the trail of more than one otter: a bitch and her accompanying young. Like the snow in winter, the drought gave

me a momentary glimpse into a hidden world. There was a conservation officer for otters responsible for the river here; he tried to monitor numbers by recording signs such as spraints, droppings left on prominent boulders as territorial markers, and advising landowners on how to make an otter-friendly habitat on the bankside. After three years in post he had decided to take a busman's holiday to Scotland, for he had yet to see an otter in the wild. I mentioned my sighting of the dog otter to the doctor at the field centre the next time I saw him, and he told me that seeing otters on the river here was a once-in-a-lifetime experience. I asked him how many times he had seen one here. Twice, he said.

My landlord told me an extraordinary story about otters living on this river, dating back around a hundred years. One of the tenant farmers had apparently turned up at the door of the big house in a state of some agitation. Come quick, m'lud, he had said when he had caught his breath, and you'd better bring your gun. The otters are killing my sheep. And it was true: the otters were indeed killing his sheep, in a fashion. A pair of cubs had constructed themselves a mudslide on the riverbank, and they were evidently having such fun chasing each other down the slide and splashing into the water that they decided to spread the joy. They began to bound around the riverside field and round up the sheep as though they were sheepdog puppies, and drive them one by one on to the slide and into the river. It is hard not to laugh at the thought of a long line of sodden, bleating sheep, bobbing downriver towards the sea, but I can understand that the farmer might not have found it quite so entertaining. History does not relate whether the landowner did in fact bring his gun, or use it, but something tells me this was not a scenario that led to a happy ending for the otter cubs.

In the same way that I surveyed nesting birds in the woods each spring, I conducted an annual survey of the river birds too. This was no gentle stroll along a riverside path – as there was no path. It entailed scrambling along vertiginous banks, clambering over fallen tree trunks, leaping over gullies or sometimes from boulder to boulder at the water's edge, climbing barbed-wire fences and picking a way through banks of nettles. The section of river I covered was only four miles or so long but it took me all day to traverse. The first mile was the heaviest going of all, the banks an overgrown jumble of boulders, the river rocky and racing. Then the river twisted and turned for a mile or two, all shifting shoals and islands in pale grey. After that it became heavily wooded to both sides; this was the part of the river closest to my cottage, which I might visit briefly on an idle day, and was one of its most secluded parts, an area never troubled by grazing sheep or cattle. The final stretch was more open and easy to negotiate; this was familiar ground, a part of the route I would always take when walking to the village, and I would finish the survey at the same spot where I always paused when on a shopping trip: a big shingly island, wide and sunny and the perfect place to end the day with a swim if the weather allowed.

Of all the birds on the river, the most visible was the

goosander. It is hard to imagine now that these were relatively recent arrivals; they took over the rivers of Wales
only in the 1970s, their range spreading rapidly from the
north. These are sawbill ducks; their long red bills are serrated for catching hold of slippery fish and look as if they
are toothed, and with their long flexible necks they have an
almost reptilian appearance. In theory they would come to
the river to breed, and in the winter head to the lakes and
estuaries of the lowlands, but in my experience a few would
stay on until October or even November, and the first arrivals for the new season would turn up as early as December,
so they were never really absent. There were far fewer in
the late autumn and early winter, though, their place as the
main threat to the fish supply being taken by the most
prominent winter visitor, the cormorant. Here were birds
that looked even more like reptiles than the goosanders,
especially when actively fishing with their whole bodies
submerged and just their black necks and yellow bills protruding from the flood water. It was strange to see birds that
I had always thought of as seabirds so far inland, but of
course to them, seawater or freshwater, a fish is a fish. Herons lurked on the banks too, patiently awaiting the unwary.
A walk to the river at any time of year would always turn
up at least a couple of herons. They would yelp and flush
awkwardly when surprised, apparently struggling to get
aloft on their huge wings. They looked too heavy to fly
with ease, but it was an illusion; they were always there
fishing in summer, even though the nearest heronry that I
knew of was at least fifteen miles away. Sawbills, cormor-
ants and herons: the most antediluvian of birds. Seeing

them all together through the mists that clung to the river in winter felt like stepping back in time, like watching dinosaurs.

The male and female goosanders could be different species; they look totally dissimilar, and have quite different life cycles. The males were brief visitors to the river; they would arrive in the winter or early spring, remaining only for the period of courtship and mating, and then they would be gone again, leaving the females to do all the work alone. The males seemed to just vanish from the river, and indeed from the whole country. For a long time it remained a mystery where they hid themselves all summer long, until they were finally discovered far, far away on the northern coasts of Norway, hiding out the moult in the deep fjords. They were much larger than the females, with big metallic-green heads and their bodies a white so pristine it was almost startling, like a shelduck out on an estuary amid the hordes of dun-coloured winter waders.

The little redheads, as the females are known, are much more finely built, their heads rufous and shaggy-crested, their bodies a delicate grey rather than white. They are shy birds, and would hear me coming along the riverbank and flush long before the mallards, flying fast on whistling wings. But once their eggs had hatched in their hidden tree-hole nests, the young would leave almost at once and follow their mother to the river, and then of course they couldn't flush without abandoning their young. The mother bird would be perpetually alert; as soon as she saw or heard me coming down the riverbank she would start swimming downstream repeatedly glancing back over her shoulder. The chicks would jump on to her back to hitch a free ride, or at least as many of them as could fit, for she would often have over ten chicks in tow. If she was not managing to increase the distance between me and her young she would suddenly switch to a new gear, flapping her wings and running through the water, churning up the river behind her like she had an outboard motor. And her brood of ducklings would race along behind her, trying to keep up, all leaving their own miniature wake in their trail, all vying to get a chance to hop up on to the safety of her back. Their tiny bodies would rise from the water as they ran, like miniature hovercraft.

Family parties would sometimes team up, and goosanders are known for having crèches, where one adult female will look after the young of another. A single female has been seen with as many as sixty young alongside her. The most I ever saw together on the river here was thirty, and that was impressive enough. As the young grew and lost their infant down, they would all take on the appearance of females, and they would remain with their mother, or their carer, until they were the same size as her and effectively indistinguishable in appearance. Only the behaviour of the female in charge would give her away. She would still be the one who led the escape downriver as soon as she heard me coming along the riverbank. It may seem odd that the quite different-looking male goosanders should start their lives resembling the females, but for waterfowl this made sense, as it made the vulnerable flightless young less visible to predators. Many of them, in their summer moult, pass through an eclipse plumage where the drakes look just like the ducks. It is as if the female's plumage is the default setting, and the male's finery a bolt-on extra.

Late spring, and the young birds were all leaving their nests. On a stone at the water's edge a kingfisher was perched, its head tipped back and its beak pointing upwards like a bittern hiding in the reeds, as if it were trying to look inconspicuous, something it was signally failing to achieve. As I drew nearer I kept expecting it to fly, but it never did; instead it fell off its stone face first into the water. It spread out its wings and sculled itself around in a semicircle until it reached its stone again, then clambered up and stood there dripping. Although I couldn't tell from the plumage, I knew this was a juvenile; the adults have red legs, while the young birds' legs are still black. I presumed that it had left the nesting burrow before it could fly and was waiting to be fed, which meant the burrow must be close indeed. Below the fringe of trees the bank dropped vertically the last few feet down to the water, which made it difficult to inspect without wading out into the river and looking back.

The kingfisher is really a bird of slow-moving lowland waterways, and by rights should have been on a list of absent friends, alongside birds such as swans and moorhens, conspicuous by their total absence. There was a long-established nesting site down by the village, where the river widened considerably and so had a more consistent depth, and this was supposedly as far upriver as the kingfishers came. But they were always to be seen on my stretch of the river too. They would return in February, and I would hear them before I saw them; that characteristic *chikeee* call. Then the bird would flash by in a jolt of impossible neon: cobalt blue and aquamarine, with an amber breast, the jewel of the river. The village birds would always nest on the same stretch of bank, for year after year, but it became clear to me that on my stretch of river the local birds would try different locations from one year to the next. It was surprisingly hard to locate their burrows on such heavily vegetated banks, though, and often they would elude me entirely.

The river kept its secrets well; it took time to unravel its mysteries. Over the course of my annual surveys I found two new breeding species for the county. It seemed unlikely that things could be overlooked in a country where every storm-driven Siberian warbler, every obscure wind-blown American sandpiper, seems to have been logged and photographed almost before it has made landfall, but perhaps it was not really so extraordinary. Perhaps it was just the nature of the place in which I had found myself: an obscure corner of the least densely populated region in Britain apart from the Scottish Highlands.

I was surprised the first time I flushed a pair of mandarin ducks from the river. These are not native birds; I knew that escapees from wildfowl collections had gone feral and set up successful colonies in the Home Counties, but it was a long, long way from there to the Cambrian Mountains. The male bird is extravagantly, almost implausibly, exotic-looking, with multicoloured plumes and crests and whiskers and sails. They are native to China, and they look it, but in fact they are under threat there, and their hope now lies in feral colonies in Europe. There had only been a

handful of stray sightings in Wales, and I assumed that
mine had been a one-off – a couple of wanderers passing
through – but not at all. I began to see them every time I
visited the same short stretch of the river. I couldn't understand why they had chosen that specific location; these are
forest ducks, and this was certainly not the most heavily
wooded part of the river. There was not just the one pair
either; I would often see five or six birds together on the
bank, or racing through the trees. They were small, agile
ducks, adept at twisting and turning as they flew at speed
between the tree trunks.

It was right at the same place on the river where I had
come across the flightless kingfisher that I flushed a female
mandarin. They are overshadowed by their garish mates
but are actually rather pretty in an understated way, mar-
bled with a pale blue-grey, and with a distinctive white
spectacle around each eye. The bird didn't take to the air
but started calling in distress and splashing in circles midstream as if injured, making a tremendous din, trying to
draw me on – a river bird's version of the plover's distraction display. It had to mean there were newborn young
with her, but they were hiding. The bottom of the bank
here had been undercut by the waters, and I lay down and
peered over the edge. I clung to a branch and leaned out as
far as I could, but the chicks must have been tucked right
under the overhang. The mother bird was getting more
and more distressed, so eventually I left her and carried on
downriver, frustrated.

Mandarins nest in tree holes; their preference is to nest
high, thirty or forty feet up, and the newborn ducklings

are known to be fearless, leaping to the ground from their nesting hole high in the trees when they are still tiny. I may not have been able to see the young birds, but I knew the mandarins were nesting now and perhaps I could still find their nest, so I returned the next day to look. The river-bank itself seemed unlikely; the trees along this stretch didn't look big enough or old enough to have any suitable holes in them. But set back a hundred yards or so from the river was a large field of very rough grazing, boggy and overgrown with alders and studded with ancient hollow oaks, so I decided that this was worth a quick look, and I would work my way through the fifteen or twenty old oaks one by one. The first tree I came to was one of the most massive, perhaps ten feet in diameter, and had a large hole in it at head height. Directly beneath the hole was a large boulder, so I climbed up on to that and leaned in. The hollow didn't go down to the base of the trunk, it was level with the entrance, so I reached around in the dark. And felt a nest. I grabbed a pinch of the soft grey down that lined the nest and pocketed it. It seemed incredible: a new breeding species for this part of the world, and I had found its nest in the first place I had looked. Of course, I had to be a little cautious: goosander down could be grey too. So I sent it off for analysis to get the official confirmation that I needed. This nest was no one-off: the following season I watched a female proudly leading a parade of young down-river.

My other find was surprising for a quite different reason. Early each year, when the main influx of goosanders arrived on the river, there would sometimes be a pair or two of red-breasted mergansers accompanying them. These are sawbill ducks too, close relatives that breed near to the coast. They are finer, smaller birds, and the male, at least, is quite distinctive, with grey flanks in comparison to the pure white of the male goosander, and of course the red breast for which it is named. But when the males left the river soon after, the redheads were much harder to distinguish. Smaller and skinnier, with a slightly more obvious shaggy crest, perhaps. One year I thought I had seen a female with her brood, but it was hard to be sure when the redheads were forever in the process of disappearing around the next bend in the river, and then the next. Then the following year, when I was on the heavily wooded section of bank nearest my home, something crashed out of the thick undergrowth at my feet and splashed down into the river. She began to circle close to the bank, flapping her wings and panicking but unable to flee, torn by conflicting impulses. From this close up there was no doubt that this bird was different from those I regularly saw. I checked the place where she had emerged; beneath the thick ground layer of riverside plants was a hidden trail, almost a green tunnel. I followed it back ten or fifteen feet to a secret hollow in the bank where eleven nearly spherical white eggs were hidden. They may be close relatives, but in this respect at least their habits differ markedly from their larger cousins. Unlike the goosanders with their tree-hole nests, the mergansers are ground nesters. Old records show that, long before goosanders moved south and took over the rivers of Wales, there were occasional sightings of mergansers on the river here. My suspicion is that they have always nested here in small numbers, but have been overlooked, and when their bigger, brassier relatives arrived, they simply merged into the crowd, and disappeared from view altogether.

As far as the woodland creatures were concerned the fringe of riverside trees along the river's length constituted a very long, thin wood. Badgers left their trails all along the bank and dug latrines to mark their territorial boundaries. Flycatchers dashed back and forth across the water. Sparrowhawks worked the beat, soaring above the treetops, then pausing to circle, then soaring, then circling again, as if they could not fly as slowly as necessary, as though they were worried they might have missed something important.

Working my way downriver through a thickly wooded section, I surprised a buzzard right at the water's edge just beginning to pluck a dead carrion crow. I must have missed the kill by seconds. The buzzard lifted off with the crow in its talons and set off across the river, but the weight must have been too much for it, for it dropped the crow midstream, and it fell with a splash right in the middle of the river. As I walked on along the riverbank the floating body stayed alongside me, matching my pace exactly and making me ponder the possibility that I had perhaps been accompanying the very same shower of raindrops for the whole day, as the landscape and the birds changed around us. After a minute or so, a second crow arrived, and began to circle and swoop over the floating body of what I had to assume was its mate, making calls of the utmost distress. It was very sad – crows pair for life. But what happened next took me aback. Over the course of the next minute or two, more crows began to race to the scene, flying in from every direction, until there were twenty or thirty of them wheeling and diving and calling above the dead bird. These are not in any way social birds, but crisis had brought them together and I felt as though I was witnessing a crow wake. And then, as suddenly as they had arrived, they all began to disperse, and it was once again only me and the black corpse drifting downriver side by side. Far above us hung a single red kite, waiting for the body to drift ashore.

With the end of the year's river-bird survey I could revert to a less structured relationship with the river. I would often head down the hill to the footbridge and position myself halfway across. From high above the water and midway between its banks I had a quite different perspective on the river and could see much further both upstream and downstream than I could from almost anywhere at the water's edge. If I had been busy that day chopping wood or digging, it was a particular pleasure to stroll to the bridge at dusk. There was a pair of semi-detached estate cottages near by, with a shared roof space that was home for a colony of long-eared bats – a colony at least ten times the size of mine. As darkness fell, the bats would come streaming out from under the eaves and hurry to the riverside and its trees, swooping and diving all around me. The river had its own bats too: Daubenton's bats, which skim the river, feeding on the midges and flies that live in the inch above the water's surface, and even snatching insects floating in the water, so that they look as if they are bouncing across the water like a skimming stone. These are not house-dwelling animals; they roost in crevices in trees, always close to water, and the university had put bat boxes in the woods all along this stretch of the river. They were much higher in the trees than the bird boxes, as is the bats' preference, high enough that they could be inspected only by ladder, and they had a narrow slot for the bats to enter rather than the round entrance hole that would have let in the birds.

The bats would swirl all around, passing within inches of me as darkness fell, their most active time. To my ears there was nothing beyond the quiet churning of the waters below me, a screaming silence, but to them there must have been a cacophony of sound. It is almost impossible to comprehend how they must perceive the world: they map everything around them, creating a mental image from sound as we create an image from light. When it was too dark to watch them any more I would set off back up the hill, and on a moonless night, with clouds to hide the stars, it could be almost pitch black. But if I kept to my regular route I would have no problem: I had my own mental map of the journey home that I had built out of memory. Time and distance, the texture of the ground beneath my feet, and its incline, aided by the slight fluctuations in the density of the darkness that would tell me whether or not I was beneath the trees.

There was something extraordinary about the bats, something apart from the obvious extraordinary things. As they circulated around me and hunted for their breakfast, they treated me no differently from how they would treat the branch of a tree: as an obstacle, not a threat. And in this respect they were different from almost every other mammal or bird. So many of my most memorable encounters with wildlife were those occasions when there was a breakdown in the natural order of things – the natural order of things being that wild creatures sense us coming a mile off, and run like hell. Those moments that felt to me like intimacy, like closeness to nature, must undoubtedly have seemed quite different to the animals involved. The injured raven in the hand. The plover with her eggs, or the mandarin with her young, each torn between conflicting impulses: the maternal instinct and the urge for self-preservation. Even the garden birds that we watch with pleasure at our bird-feeders are in a state of conflict: safety or hunger. When the weather is at its worst, more and more birds throng to the table, because the alternative to facing their fear is starvation. It is easy to sentimentalize nature, to forget that the prevailing forces at work – besides the urge to hold a territory and find a mate – are hunger and fear. Our position in nature is anomalous: we are the pole predator and almost everything fears us, while most other predators in the animal kingdom are themselves running scared. The sparrowhawk fears the goshawk just as the chaffinch fears the sparrowhawk, and with good reason; when the goshawks move in, the number of sparrowhawks inevitably falls.

In the Western world our relationship with nature is unnatural. Hunger is historical, and any animals that could have been a threat to us, the wolves and bears, have been either eliminated or pushed into ever more remote outposts. I could walk in the forest at night and fear nothing, because there is nothing worse to fear than the possibility of bumping into a tree in the darkness. Close encounters with wildlife are very different when the wildlife you are watching would sooner eat you than run away from you.

It was the end of the season and I was going down into the valley, to a hidden vantage point overhung by trees on a secluded, wooded reach of the river. I approached perpendicular to the river so that I could go directly to my chosen place without having to walk the bank and risk disturbing anything. I got comfortable and prepared myself for a long wait. After all those months of crashing along the riverbank with my clipboard in hand it was time to enjoy the simple benefits of sitting quietly and seeing what happens. There was nothing there to see as I arrived, and that was surely good, for it meant there was nothing to disturb. It was a pleasant, sunny day on a narrow stretch of river where the trees on each side reached out and shaded at least half of the water's surface. The waters here ran fast and shallow, their gentle babbling the ideal accompaniment for a long vigil. It is difficult to remain still for long periods, but I'd had practice: all those evenings out watching the badgers and the woodcocks, the rainy days sat on my doorstep beneath the shelter of my porch just watching the world go by, and most of all a multitude of nights sat doing nothing by the flickering fire.

I didn't have long to wait. The kingfisher announced that it was coming; they always seem to call as they patrol the river. It perched on the overhanging branch of the tree right beside me, and I could tell that in spite of its glorious plumage this bird was a juvenile – it had the same black legs as the flightless bird I had found not far from here. From that second on the river seemed to be alive with king-fishers, flying past repeatedly in ones and twos. There was no way of guessing how many there were as they flew up and down, back and forth. The youngster in the tree next to me took off after a passing bird, but was soon replaced by another that settled directly opposite me on a branch that hung low over the water. This new arrival had the bright red legs of an adult. In fact, I could tell that this was the female, for though their plumage is indistinguishable, the male's bill is all black, while the female has a distinctive red lower mandible.

As I watched, a nuthatch that had been hopping around the hazels near by found itself a nut. It had done well to find one as I never managed to get my hands on any myself; the grey squirrels took all the hazelnuts while they were still small and green. The nuthatch carried its find over to the tree beside me, wedged the nut into a crevice in its bark, and began to hammer away at it. It was remarkably noisy at such close range. I could see it out of the corner of my eye but didn't want to make a move – it was so close. It surprised me that the kingfisher wasn't distracted by the noise, but it was obviously a familiar sound and she ignored it entirely, her attention focused instead on the water drift-ing by beneath her perch. And then she dived. A second or two later she was back on her perch with a fish in her beak. A perfect view of a kingfisher fishing, like something out of a documentary, soundtracked by the nuthatch on rhythm, and the river on melody. Over the course of the next ten minutes the kingfisher caught three more fish. The first two she ate herself, the third she carried off for her young. There was a lull for a while – the kingfisher had gone and the nuthatch too – and then a loud piercing call and a kingfisher shot upriver, flying low and fast. Right on its tail, a rather optimistic buzzard was in hot pursuit, trying its hardest to keep up without its wingtips getting wet. A minute later, the kingfisher returned alone, quite unruffled.

A family of goosanders was making its way upriver to where I was waiting. It made a change to see them swimming towards me for once instead of sailing away. By this late stage in the season, the young birds were able to fly, and were virtually impossible to tell apart from the mother bird. Perhaps she was still a fraction larger, her crest still a little shaggier; and she was still the boss. There were thirteen in this family, and they were fishing in an extraordinary fashion that I had never witnessed before. They were spread in a dead-straight line across the entire width of the river, which was perhaps forty feet at this point, the mother in the very middle of the river and six of her young to either side of her, perfectly evenly spaced. They reminded me of a line of pheasant-beaters. All had their necks stretched flat out across the surface of the water before them, with their eyes just underwater, for some of the time at least. Every few seconds they would scuttle forward with a flick of their big red feet and snatch at a fish. Splash and grab. Only the few birds in midstream actually needed to dive, so shallow was the water here at this moment. As they all filed past me, the nearest bird was barely ten feet away, but it saw nothing; only noise or movement would have alerted them and caused their usual panic.

Soon after they had passed me, the birds turned and began to drift downriver, falling out of line as the faster water midstream sent a few of them surging ahead. I thought that was the end of the show, but not at all; after fifty yards they all turned back towards me again, assumed their positions and began to work their beat. Just as they reached me, they must have encountered a whole shoal of tiny fish, for the half-dozen or so birds furthest across the river from me suddenly formed themselves into a tight semicircle, almost wing to wing, and pushed towards the far shore. I had no idea that birds could perform such co-ordinated teamwork when they hunted; each bird seemed to know the exact position to take, while those on my side of the river held their posts, undistracted by the feeding frenzy taking place in the shallows opposite. Once again, as soon as they had passed the shallow rapids where I had positioned myself, they turned and drifted back down the river just as they had before, to regroup and begin one more pass. This was to be the final time; perhaps they had used up everything the river had to offer here, or perhaps their hunger had just been sated. They broke rank and gathered in a cluster around the mother bird in the middle of the river, directly in front of me, as if for a debrief. They held their position perfectly, swimming so that their pace matched the current exactly, and began to preen themselves with their brilliant red serrated bills. Time had stood still and I felt invisible; I could scarcely believe what I had seen, and that I had the shyest birds on the river still no more than twenty feet away, oblivious to my presence. And then one by one they finished their preening, folded up their long necks like coiling snakes, tucked their slender bills under their wings, and slept.

9. *What Remains*

Summer came to a reluctant end. The buzzards and the kites circled lazily on the thermals, rising high, and the ravens were out with their three young, rolling and calling continually. But the hillside was still mostly silent in the sunshine, and the songbirds were still hidden away in the moult. The first to emerge was a party of mistle thrushes, sleek and glossy in their new plumage, which seemed to have adopted my patch of hillside as their hunting ground. There were at least thirty of them, along with a handful of camp followers, a few chaffinches and a couple of warblers. For four days I watched them closely whenever they were in sight. I knew that thirty fat thrushes would not have attracted my attention alone, and the thrushes seemed to know this too; they fed on the ground but were twitchy and nervous, and would stay close to the trees, ready to dive for cover at the slightest provocation.

On the afternoon of the fourth day the moment came. I was out at my woodpile chopping logs when I saw the flock suddenly lift from the bottom of the front field. The flock flashed light and dark, light and dark, as the birds twisted and turned in sudden jerky movements, like winter dunlin on the estuary, but their hunter hung fast, its long tail swinging from side to side with each check, each sudden corner. The goshawks were back from their summer holidays. This hawk was out of luck though, for the raven family was near at hand over Penlan Wood and decided to intervene. The two adults dived right in and began to harry the hawk, while the young held back, for dealing with a hungry hawk was clearly an adult matter. After the first few passes, the hawk dived back, and the thrushes were able to slip away and make their escape during the brief distraction. And that was the last time I saw this particular flock of thrushes on my hillside that autumn; now the hawks were on the hill it was no longer safe for them there.

September, and the sun of summer lingered on. There were still a few wild flowers in the garden: the last fading yellow of the St John's wort, and a straggle of red campion. There was a surprise tap at the window – a bumblebee that returned again and again to headbutt the glass and would not take no for an answer. There were still butterflies too, red admirals and painted ladies, though the first of my winter tortoiseshells was already asleep on my pantry ceiling. As my harvest began, the birds most in evidence were those that were busy with a harvest of their own. There was the constant *tippy-tippy-tap* of the nuthatches as they gathered acorns and cracked them open. The jays were out in force too, busily putting together their own winter stockpile, looping from tree to tree. They would drop from their perch, skim along the ground, and swoop up when they reached the next oak along, perching at the same height they had started from, making their journey twice as long as if they had flown straight and level.

The number of bats emerging from my loft at dusk was at its peak now that the year's young were on the wing.

One morning I went into my woodshed to find that the young bats had moved in overnight. They had obviously decided that they were getting too old for a nursery roost, and were having their first sleepover party. There were probably nearly twenty of them; it was hard to tell for they had all clustered together into a furry brown football hanging from a roof-beam just above my head. These were long-eared bats: tiny, extraordinary-looking creatures, with ears proportionately far larger than those of a rabbit or hare. They were handsome creatures in their own strange way, with sharp foxy faces instead of the snub noses of most bats. They slept with their ears tucked neatly under their folded wings, but they had heard me come in and began to unfold their ears and open their eyes. They started to yawn, their mouths wide in a silent scream. It looked as though they were trying to intimidate me with their minuscule pointy teeth, but in fact they were echolocating me, and it made me wonder how I looked in sound, in the bats' strange synaesthetic world. When they started to flex their wings, I beat a retreat, for I didn't want them risking flying outside in broad daylight. I could manage for a day without my woodshed, and I knew they would have no intention of staying there for the longer term – it was far too bright and exposed for them.

The first mixed flocks began to gather: tits and finches and goldcrests, with a scattering of migrant birds such as pied flycatchers and willow warblers, which I would see only a few more times before they set off for warmer climes. Down on the lanes the swallows were gathering, skittish and restless; one by one they would settle on the wires in a long line, then suddenly all take off again as if on a secret signal. The house martins were flocking too, high above. One year the martins came to my cottage, swooping up under the eaves with their beaks filled with mud that they would use as plaster, but they never completed their nests, and never returned. Perhaps one day. The mountain ashes, the rowans, were so heavily laden with berries that their branches drooped like weeping willows, showing the pale silvery undersides of their leaves. And the woods were beginning to look scorched, with just the outermost leaves of the canopy starting to turn, as if a flame had passed over the trees and singed them. There was autumn song in the woods: robins, virtually the only birds so determinedly territorial that they would set up a winter territory for themselves and not just a breeding territory. It was nice to hear, though – it felt like an echo of spring.

Down on the river there were still kingfishers and the last of the goosanders. And there were huge gatherings of mallards. In the winter there would be distinctly separate male and female flocks, but for now it was impossible to tell them apart for they all still looked almost identical in their eclipse plumage. In among the flocks were the occasional smaller ducks too: mandarins, also in eclipse, looking as if they were hiding their true colours, trying to blend in with the crowd. All along the banks were stands of Indian balsam, still bearing a few pink-and-white flowers like oversized snapdragons. In sheltered places the plants reached four or five feet high and as I brushed past them the tightly wound seed pods would explode, peppering me with tiny black seeds. They would be propelled several feet; some would end up in the river to start new colonies downstream, while others would collide with other plants and set them off too in a chain reaction, until the whole colony was trembling.

I sat on a large mossy boulder the size of a small car that protruded into the river, watching the water roll by and enjoying the autumn sunshine; I knew there would not be many more opportunities to sit in the sun for months to come. Every breeze that blew sent a shower of golden coins fluttering down on to the water, the yellowing leaves of the birches that were already beginning to fall. A single bat, a pipistrelle I thought, was following the river, and I wondered what it was doing out and about in broad daylight. A male sparrowhawk was working its beat above the riverside trees: soar, circle, soar, circle. Over in the big wood on the hillside opposite, where I knew that sparrowhawks nested each year, I could see three hawks above the distant trees, the year's young still not dispersed. These birds needed to be wily; it was almost provocative how close this nesting site was to the keeper's cottage and the rearing pens. But today everybody seemed to be out enjoying the sun regardless. They all suddenly melted into the trees as another, much larger, bird came cruising over the horizon of trees: one of the newly returned goshawks.

I made my way back up the hillside in the gloaming after my afternoon at the river, and noticed a mound of fresh sawdust on the track at my feet as I approached the edge of the beech wood. I looked up at the stone-dead horizontal bough that overhung the track above my head. There was a perfectly round hole in it, and as the branch was not thick enough for a deeper hole, I could see its occupant framed: a great spotted woodpecker, a male, its beak pointed straight up as though it were trying to ignore me. It would have been no surprise to find a woodpecker roosting in an old nesting site but I had no idea one would go to the trouble of excavating a brand-new hole solely for use as a winter roost. It would be in residence most times that I passed over the next few weeks, until a storm sent the old rotten bough crashing to the ground.

The weather held for the harvest moon. As the sun set, a huge, bulbous, blood-red balloon rose on the opposite horizon, smearing the low cloud carmine. By the time of the next full moon, the hunter's moon, everything had begun to change. The season of fog and wind. There were two distinct fogs here: a rising fog and a falling fog. The first of these would settle above the river on a clear cold night, and would bring me those bright mornings of such breathtaking beauty that as I looked out over the rolling ocean of foam beneath me I would think: forget everything else, it was worth coming here for this alone. In a falling fog, the clouds would drop over the mountains and envelop me. All would be still and grey and washed-out, but when the clouds were on the move, this fog could have its magic too. As I walked on the hill, cut off from everything, with bands and belts of denser cloud drifting in procession through the canopy of the pine woods, the landscape looked primal and mysterious. A dark beauty rather than the brilliant beauty of the rising fog.

The first frost came. When I went to get water for

washing one morning there was the first thin disc of ice floating on the surface beneath the lid of the water-butt; when I tapped it with the edge of my jug it snapped crisply in two, like a poppadom. That first frost always felt like a turning point; there would be no going back now. It brought the winter flocks. A huge flock of siskins, over a hundred of them, was working the line of alders that trailed down the hill, following the shallow gulley of the seasonal stream that originated from the overflow to my well. All summer long the siskins lived deep in the plantations and I would seldom see them, but in winter they emerged en masse from the conifers, were joined by birds from the north, and lived almost wholly on the alder seeds. When at the tail end of winter their food supply finally ran dry, they would turn to my bird table to see them through. There were goldfinches too, a tinkling flock of fifty or so, that fluttered from thistle-head to thistle-head, and a flock of at least twenty yellowhammers. One year the yellowhammers spent the entire winter within sight of my cottage. If I could not see them out in my front fields, I would wander up the track and look up the hill to see them in the back field. They were like my mascots for the winter. At night they would roost in the fruit tree in the garden behind my bird table. I would wake early on a dull, misty morning, everything grey and blurred and indistinct, and look out the slotted window of my living room to see them, bright yellow flags dotted all over the tree. A string of yellow bunting that almost glowed through the drizzle and the mist, like Christmas-tree lights.

At the very top of an alder on the edge of Penlan Wood was perched a small bird of prey. A male sparrowhawk, I thought at first, but its posture was too upright, and it was in too prominent a position. Perhaps a kestrel; I had watched a pair of kestrels earlier that day on the hillside by the ravens' nest, hovering above the collapsing bracken, working systematically and in tandem, each leapfrogging over the other to methodically cover the entire ridge line. As I approached the edge of Penlan Wood to try to get a closer view, the bird flushed. I should have been able to tell if it was a falcon in flight, but it turned and raced out of sight over the trees. Sometimes they are gone before you can be sure what they are. But this time the bird returned and settled at the top of a spruce, and now I was nearer I had enough information to be certain: it was a female merlin. It is not very often you get given a second shot at an identification. The moors, where she had come from, would be lifeless now; the pipits and larks and wheatears would all be gone. The merlin would spend her winter in the lowlands or most likely on the coast, and she would be just passing through here.

I saw her again the following day. I was visiting my postbox, and there she was, high above the hillside over the woods, harassing a buzzard determinedly. She looked so tiny way up there, and the comparison between her slender curved wings and the buzzard's square solidity made her look more like a swallow mobbing a sparrowhawk. She was relentless in her pursuit of the buzzard, and though she had only arrived on the hill the day before it was as though she was taking ownership. She stayed on the hillside all month; I kept thinking she had left and then I would see her dashing by again. The next year there was no sign of her, or any other merlins, but eventually the time came again for one to stop over for a while on its way from the moors. It became a feature of my autumns: I would keep an eye out for the merlins, in hope if not in expectation.

October, and the trees were in full fall. The larch woods were gilded, the beech woods bronzed, and as for the oak woods, well, each and every tree seemed to be a harlequin of every possible autumn hue. Only the ashes would disappoint, their greenery just fading a little before starting to fall. And as soon as the time had come for the ashes to start shedding their leaves, the jackdaw ash on the rocks behind the cottage would give up its struggle; one day it would be in full leaf, the next I would look and it would be totally bare. It would always be the first. All the others would take weeks to surrender to the inevitable and become leafless save for the bunches of keys at their tips, which the wood-pigeons would come and unpick, swinging from the slender twigs with surprising dexterity.

The winds came, and blew in gust after gust of redwings, huge numbers of them but in discrete flocks of twenty or thirty travelling at impossible speed with the winds hard behind them. They came all day long, newly blown in from Scandinavia, and gathered down in the valley. On a bright, sunny afternoon, I followed the flocks down the hillside. Through the old oaks at the bottom of my front fields I paused and sat on the remains of a long-abandoned tractor that gave me a fine view over the patchwork quilt of the woodland canopy below me lit up by the sun. Deep in the drifts of leaf litter beneath the trees, a cornucopia of toadstools and mushrooms would be fighting their way through the mulch. Decay has its own fecundity. There was the white barkless skeleton of a solitary tree in the field by me, and in it were perched a pair of kites. There was a third kite too, flying over the stand of oaks I had come through. The perched birds flew up, and the three birds all made passes at each other, swoops and circles just above the trees at only twenty or thirty feet above me, before settling again. They seemed not to mind me being there watching them, and their repeated sallies didn't appear to serve any purpose; they were simply out enjoying the sun and the wind like I was.

A goshawk was flying over the streamside woods, following the path of the stream uphill and straight into the thrust of the wind. He would soar for a while, then veer upwards until he stalled. For a while he would hang suspended, motionless, his broad wings outspread as if in crucifixion. Then the wind would take him, and he would be blown backwards. It was like he was daring himself; at the last possible moment, just as it seemed he would be dashed into the trees, he would flip himself around, make a tight circle, and go back to soaring over the dingle. As he passed over the mottled woods, redwings would dash out of the cover of the trees below and race up to him. As soon as they reached him they would drop immediately back down to safety. There must have been thousands of the newly arrived redwings sheltering in the canopy, and this pattern followed the hawk's progress all along the length of the valley woods. It was like a Mexican wave of rising and falling birds rippling across the treetops, and the goshawk was surfing that wave in fine style.

The winds turned storm force. I lay awake that night listening to the howling outside. There was a whole language of wind out there; the gusts seemed to be coming from different directions at once, each with its own voice. I could hear the clattering of the roof tiles and wondered how many I would have to replace. With luck they would hit the ground without shattering; I had no spares left and was already having to use tiles with their corners chipped off. If the ash on the rocks behind the cottage was ever going to come down and take my roof with it, it would have been on that night.

Eventually I lapsed into a fitful sleep, and when I woke the next day the storm had blown itself out. I went outside to check on the damage, and several of the ash trees in front of the cottage had lost large boughs, but the jackdaw ash was undamaged. Perhaps because it was the only one that had lost all its leaves already, the wind had just blown straight through it as if it had not been there. In the fields both above and below me trees had fallen, but, quite noticeably, it was not the hollow trees that had been overpowered but the sturdier-looking solid ones. There seemed no order to it; some had fallen north, some south, some to face uphill and some down. Their falling had wrenched great root plates out of the ground, ten or fifteen feet across, and where the roots at the bottom of these were still embedded in the ground the trees would not necessarily die; they would now grow horizontally instead of vertically. In the woods the trees that had fallen were much more likely to have snapped right off; surrounded by competition, they would have had to grow faster to reach for the light, and would be slender for their height. The biggest victim was a massive oak on the bank of the stream. As if the wind had blown directly down from above and crushed it, its trunk had shattered downwards rather than crossways, and it had fallen in every direction at once, like a chocolate orange.

That afternoon I walked up to the summit cairn of my mountain, and looked out to the north. Though it had been eerily still further down, it was still bright and gusty and bracing up here. On the hillside facing me across the valley to the north, almost an entire small plantation had been clear-felled by the winds, and from here it looked like a tangle of matchsticks. It had blown out from the centre, and all that remained was a fringe of sturdier trees all around its periphery: the outline of a wood.

Two autumns in a row, hares came and bred in the overgrown field in front of the cottage, around my well. Hares were not at all common here; they didn't like the closely cropped improved grassland of the hill farms, and although hares are active in the daytime and therefore easier to see than most mammals, sometimes weeks would go by without my seeing a single one. They are tough creatures that live out in the open in all seasons, all weathers. They don't rely on burrows or nests for shelter and protection but on their ability to outrun predators. And they are fast: if they lived in town they could easily break the speed limit. As a child I would see them in large numbers when I walked on the marshes. In spring I would make a point of going to look for them so I could watch them boxing: the traditional spectacle of the mad March hares. At that time their fights were thought to be between the males, known as jacks, competing for the attention of the females, known as jills; now it is believed that it is actually the females, to our eyes indistinguishable from the males, fighting off the premature or unwanted attentions of the males. But here the jack was in no danger of getting his crown broken. The problem for the females here was not fighting off unwanted suitors but finding a mate, any mate, in the first place.

Hares can breed at any time of the year, and the young leverets have to be as hardy as the adults, for they are left in a form, a hollow in the grass that offers no more protection than the bare scrape of the nest of a wader. Their defence from predators is to stay very, very still until they have no alternative but to run. The fields of sheep-grazing didn't offer enough cover for them, but the field around my well was becoming visibly more and more overgrown year on year, as bracken spread from the edge of Penlan Wood, along with banks of sedge where the field was boggy, and nettles and thistles in the drier ground around the rocky remains of Penlan Farm. Sheep still passed through, but the field was growing steadily more marginal and unappetizing for them, and steadily more attractive for wildlife. I had no idea how many leverets were in the field, for they were all hidden in separate spots, for safety's sake, but for a whole month of each of those two successive autumns it seemed as though whenever I walked down to my well, little hares would explode from every stand of nettles, every clump of sedge.

They didn't all make it. One year, on the twenty-foot slab of exposed rock beside my fruit tree, where the mosses and liverworts grew, I found the bloody stump of a young hare's hind leg. Dropped there by a buzzard, I supposed, or perhaps by a hawk. I was fairly sure it had been carried there rather than killed there, as there was no sign of plucked fur, or any other remains. Just that one solitary paw. The next year, I found a skinned leveret on the track in front of the cottage. The skin was inside out, with the fur facing inwards like the wool on a sheepskin coat. The head had been eaten, but all four paws were snapped off and still attached. It was a neat job, the work of a badger, I thought, rather than a fox. Badgers didn't often approach this close to the cottage – only once had I gone out at night and surprised one at my fence – but this drama had taken place right outside my window, in the deep darkness while I slept, and I had not been disturbed.

One late-autumn day I opened the back door to fetch some water, and there was a young hare sat on my back step. Save for the twitching of its nose, it froze in position as if I had surprised it as it was about to knock. It was already the size of a full-grown rabbit, and its black-tipped ears were longer than any rabbit's would ever be. I stood there and waited for it to flush. After a while I began to doubt that it would, and squatted down to its level for a closer look, eye to eye. It stared back at me apparently unconcerned, chewing silently, with bulging eyes that were such a rich golden colour they were almost orange, with black depths like the keyhole of a door to another world. I tried to imagine what might be going on in its mind, whether it might be ill or injured, and considered what might happen if I tried to pick it up. It seemed like a risky survival strategy, to trust in your camouflage when you are sitting on a doorstep, and I wondered if its sibling had done the same when it had been caught out by a badger on my track. As I touched the little hare, it burst into life and raced away at incredible speed, turning on a pin at the corner of the cottage. I dashed after it and was in time to see it clear my drystone wall, fence and all: a perfect arc of perhaps twenty feet. The next day the young hares had gone from my front field, scattered. They were close to adulthood now, ready to begin their wanderings, and I wouldn't see a single hare again until Christmas.

That was my fourth autumn at the cottage, and I felt that I had the measure of life there. All my systems were in place for the months of austerity to come. My woodshed was well stocked with drying logs; what had needed harvesting from the garden vegetable patches was stored away in the pantry; I had my thirty jars of jam, my selection of pickled and dried wild mushrooms. But there are some things you cannot prepare for. There was another storm coming: my own personal fall. I became ill. Of course I had been ill at the cottage before with colds and fevers – though admittedly not as frequently as when I was surrounded by people and more exposed to infection – and I would just keep myself warm and weather it out. This was something else altogether: a whole range of symptoms that I struggled to make any sense of, or even, to begin with, to recognize as signs of illness.

At night I found myself lying awake for hours, tossing and turning restlessly, or staring up into the dark, waiting until I could begin to make out the cracks in the ceiling and could justify to myself that it was now daytime and I could reasonably get up. I no longer slept for more than an hour or two each night, and, though I might feel physically exhausted in the daytime as a result, I never felt tired enough to sleep then. Instead, I felt jittery and on edge; I twitched and fiddled and fidgeted and couldn't sit still for a minute. I became aware of a constant nervous tremor, like a vibration that ran right through me, to the bone. And I became almost fearful, of nothing. It felt as though there was a dark shadow that kept falling over me from somewhere behind me, from something just out of view.

This was not the self I thought I knew. I simply could not accept me as this bag of nerves; in my mind, at least, I had always been the calmest and most even-tempered person in the room, someone who could cope with whatever life threw at them. A friend once asked me if I didn't sometimes get afraid, living the way I did. I was bemused, and I couldn't begin to understand what he was talking about. He had to spell it out for me: I lived all alone on a remote mountainside, far from any help, in a creaky old house with cobwebs and flickering candlelight and a loft full of bats. And I had to admit that it had never crossed my mind to think of it like that; it hadn't occurred to me that people might consider any of these elements something you could be afraid of. To my eyes it was just me, at home, getting on with my life.

But now I began to consider something I would never have thought possible previously: that I was having some kind of nervous breakdown. I looked at my life to see if there were any hidden points of stress that might have had this effect on me, and I could find nothing. My life might have been physically demanding at times, but that was as far as it went; the way I saw it, I was leading a life without any stress whatsoever. I began to wonder whether it might in fact be the total absence of stress that was the problem.

In the end, what took me to the doctor was the realization that I was losing weight, a lot of weight, and not for want of eating; I had been behaving like a squirrel getting ready to hibernate for the winter, eating four or five substantial meals a day and still being hungry at the end of them. I wasn't sure how long this had been going on, and it probably took longer for me to recognize the change than it would have done for anyone else. I never looked in a mirror and of course had no bathroom scales – I didn't even have a bathroom. Nor did I have anyone around to tell me I looked different, so it was only when I noticed that my ribs were protruding that I took note of what was happening. I set off down the hill, over the suspension bridge across the river and to the main road, where I hitched up-valley to the town where I was registered with a doctor. This was not the town I occasionally went to for shopping, but it was a more straightforward hitch, along just one road. I had a good relationship with my doctor; when I had first gone to register he had seen my name and come out to see if it was really me. We had been school friends, and our very different paths in life had ended up delivering us both to the same place, at the same time. I didn't know quite what I was going to say to him when I saw him this time.

He was able to make a provisional diagnosis before I had even arrived at his surgery. He saw me from his window, walking up the driveway in jeans and a T-shirt. As he pointed out to me later, everyone else was already dressed in overcoats and scarves, hats and gloves. I had been vaguely aware of this myself, but had assumed this was because my time on the hill had made me hardy, while others had gone soft from years of central heating and running hot water. He took my temperature – way too high – and my pulse – way too fast, fluttering like the heart of a bird. Then he showed me the swelling in my neck where my thyroid gland was swollen to twice its normal size. There followed batteries of tests, visits to hospital, stays in hospital, and though I was able to recover without needing an operation, I required heavy doses of drugs over many months to reduce the inflammation.

It shook me to the core. I had thought I knew exactly who I was, but it turned out that a minute chemical imbalance in my body could turn my whole life out of balance and change me into a different person altogether. We tend to think of the self as something fixed, the bottom line, but it seemed now to be the most fragile of constructs. It was not until my metabolic hormones started to regain their natural equilibrium that I began to drift back towards becoming the relaxed person I had always known. So perhaps this was my default setting after all, the place I came back to when all was well with the world; perhaps this is as much as we can hope for, that the person we find when we come looking for ourselves is conditional at best.

That autumn, however, while I was ill, all my certainties blew away with the falling leaves. I was not as independent as I had thought, not as self-sufficient. The drug treatment I was on left me weak and lacking in energy; the walk to the village shop felt like an ordeal; I didn't have enough concentration to keep my journal, or even to read. I had friends that would have happily lent me some support, but they were far away. I had made no effort to create any sort of support network where I was. Quite the reverse: as the years had gone by I had isolated myself further and further as I grew more and more habituated to the solitary life. I had made one friend on the estate within walking distance, the sort of friend I could drop in on when passing by, and my landlord and landlady would generously offer to take me into town if I needed a shopping run or a hospital visit. But other than that I was on my own.

It would have been the sensible time to leave the cottage, but I didn't do that. I would be there for another eighteen months yet. Perhaps it was stubbornness, but I wanted to jump rather than be pushed. The winter to come would not be the hardest in terms of the harshness of its weather, but it would undoubtedly be my hardest test. I tried to keep to my habit of going out each day, even if the walk to my postbox was as far as I could manage, or perhaps the river on a good day. Otherwise I would move slowly through my day, doing what I had to do to keep myself alive. Fire, water, food, sleep. I was not unhappy. From my window seat I watched the world outside, and the struggle for survival that was played out daily on my bird table.

What remains if you peel away all those things that help you think you know who you are? If one by one you strip away your cultural choices, the validation you get from the company of your peer group, the tools you use for communication? Then what is left behind? If you had asked me that three or four years earlier, when I was just arriving at Penlan, I imagine that I would have guessed: your true self. But I soon found that in fact I rapidly became less and less self-aware; my attention was elsewhere, on the outside. And now that circumstances had forced me to look inward once again, it was to discover that there was perhaps no fixed self to find. So what was there instead? Now, more than ever, I had the sense that my life was not so very different from that of the birds fluttering on my bird-feeder, as though a boundary between us had been broken.

Though I could not be persuaded to leave the hill for my months of convalescence, there was one respect in which I gave in to pressure: I got myself a phone. With no electricity or water at the cottage, it seemed anomalous that there was a long trail of telegraph poles already in place, spaced along the top edge of Penlan Wood, then sloping off down the hill to meet the lanes by my postbox. If those poles had not already been there then connection would have been prohibitively expensive, as nowadays you have to pay per pole – and it took an awful lot of them to link me up to the line that ran alongside the lanes – but long ago, when telecommunications were about to be privatized and it was the final chance to take advantage of the flat fee for connection to any address, a line had astutely been strung to every building on the estate, in case it was ever needed. So I had only to pay for the reconnection of an existing service, even though it had never been used before.

I took the decision with a great deal of reluctance; it felt like I was letting myself down. I had always been blithely confident, believing that nothing could possibly go wrong. I would happily scamper about on my shaky woodpile, brandishing my chainsaw and wearing no protective clothing whatsoever, serenely certain that everything would be fine, everything would always be fine. Even though the farmer's accident with the tractor many years before had proved conclusively that here we were beyond yelling distance of any assistance, I had always felt myself charmed, exempt. But everything had changed with my illness. I could no longer convince myself or others that nothing could go wrong; something had already gone wrong, and it was me.

It took a team of telephone engineers days to get me reconnected. The wire had broken in several places on its way down the hill, and overhanging trees had to be manicured and cut back to give the cable a free run. On the first day the team made the mistake of trying to get to me from the lane by my postbox by driving their Land Rover along the old cart track. It cost them as much to get the farmer to tow them out of the mud with his tractor as it would cost me to get my phone installed. On the second day they came better prepared; they brought two vehicles and drove up to me along the track from the farm, following my directions. One of them still managed to get bogged down in the thick mud of the rutted track in front of the cottage, but they had thought to bring a chain to use as a tow rope, and after much pushing and shoving and spinning of tyres in the churning mud they managed to save themselves the embarrassment of having to go cap in hand to the farmer for the second day running. I don't know what they must have thought of the way I lived my life. Eventually the job was done and they were gone, leaving nothing but the mess they had made of my track, and my connection to the rest of the world in the shape of one thin wire.

I sat by my fire and tried not to keep glancing over at the phone in the window, the elephant in the room. It lurked on its windowsill, glowering at me reprovingly, ready to shatter the silence and remind me how I had surrendered my higher ideals. Of course I knew it didn't really lurk, or glower, or reprove; it was only a phone, after all. It wasn't even about to ring; I hadn't plugged it in and had no intention of doing so. I would use it for outgoing calls only. But any difference it made to me practically was far outweighed by its psychological impact. My life felt less isolated now, less remote. It felt like the first step of my rehabilitation into the world of men.

As autumn turned to winter I retrenched, withdrew further inside myself. My recovery was slow, and my life became centred around the conservation of energy. Even the walk to the postbox felt like too much of an ordeal. My overcoat came off only when I slept. I felt ill and I felt tired, but I knew what was wrong with me now and I knew that I would recover – it was just a matter of patience. I could wait it out; the days would lengthen again, the sap would rise, and my strength would return. It was all a part of the same cycle, it was all good.

I had not planned to mark Christmas that year, but when I woke on Christmas Eve and looked out to see that several inches of snow had fallen overnight I relented. Of course I already knew there had been a snowfall without having to look out; I would always know from the moment I woke, before I had even opened my eyes. From the snow-light on my eyelids, from the muffled quality of the hush. Even the cold air on my skin was its own peculiar kind of cold. I wrapped up warm and took my bow saw from its hook on the woodshed wall. I would head up the back field to the pine wood at the hilltop ridge. At the northern edge of this wood was a handful of stunted spruces that would never amount to much in such an exposed position. There would be no harm in cutting one, and there was something appealing about marking the depths of winter by bringing a tree into your home. Not just the conifer, but the holly and ivy and mistletoe too, every plant in the woods that stayed green all winter long. It seemed an expression of hope that better days were coming, an act of defiance against the long dark nights.

The snow had not long stopped falling. It was pristine, an open book, an unmarked page. It felt festive: deep and crisp and even. I waded out into it and set off up the back field, in the perfect stillness, the perfect silence. About halfway up the field my foot kicked against a clod hidden beneath the snow. The clod burst into the air, showering me with snow, as if in a surprise snowball attack. It was a hare, the first I had seen since the hare on my back doorstep months before. Perhaps it was even the same animal, there was no way of telling. The hare raced away up the hillside at incredible speed, unhindered by the incline or the deep snow, its forelegs and its hind legs criss-crossing with each bound. I would be able to follow its trail all the way up the hill to the pine wood where I was headed. I looked down at the little impression in the snow where the animal had been sleeping; I squatted down, took off my glove, and felt the hare's warmth still in the hollow of the grass. It must have settled there at the end of the day, in the middle of the open field. And in the night, when the snow had begun to fall, it had not gone to seek shelter, but had carried on sleeping regardless. As the snowflakes settled on its fur, as the inches of snow slowly banked up over it, it had just stayed right where it was.

Epilogue

Penlan Wood is long gone, and I had a hand in its demise. The estate supplied me with a brush cutter, and gave me a season to take out the understorey in preparation for the wood being sold for clear-felling the following year. Before the spruces grew up, the wood must have been an impenetrable thicket of rhododendrons, like the streamside thicket over the old bridge where I liked to sit of an evening. As the spruces had grown tall they had starved the rhododendrons of light, and all that remained of them in the dark heart of the wood were their brittle skeletons. But all around the wood's fringes they had continued to flourish, and encircled it with a ten-foot-thick belt of tangled branches that was hard to breach. They overhung the wire fence all round the wood, and they overhung the gulley along my side of the plantation where the woodcocks sheltered under their leaves. Rhododendrons are not native, and they are invasive, so they receive a lot of criticism, but their flowers are glorious and they reminded me of the beautiful montane forests of the Himalayas, which is where they originate from, and that felt like a good place to be reminded of.

The next year the team moved in. The timber was shipped out from the bottom of the wood, so I never saw the foresters, and at no point did they need to come along my track. I think they got a good deal; as it had never been thinned they got a lot more timber than they had bargained for. On the day the chainsaws started, a big mixed flock of woodland birds emerged and spent all day milling around my cottage. Tits and finches, woodpeckers, treecreepers, nuthatches, wrens and robins and goldcrests: between fifty and a hundred birds in all. Who would have thought that those few acres of unappealing spruce would have been hiding such large numbers of small birds? The farmer asked the loggers to leave a line of trees at the top of the wood to act as a shelter belt for his sheep. They left rather a generous swathe of mature trees that included the sparrowhawks' nesting site of at least the past three years, but the change was too much for the hawks and they elected to move elsewhere.

When the job was done, the hill looked bare and my cottage was exposed to the westerly wind. For the first time I could hear a cock crowing and a sheepdog barking from a farmhouse on the next hillside along. The logging team had been asked to leave any hardwoods and take just the spruce. There were a few standards, tall and strong, mostly around the edges of the wood where they had managed to get enough light, and a cluster of scrubby willows around a spring-fed boggy hollow in its middle. But the majority of the fifty or so trees, predominantly birch, that were scattered about the ruins of the plantation were spindly and frail, unnaturally tall and thin where they had raced for the light against the fast-growing conifers. They had no future; with the first strong wind most either snapped off or bowed right down so that their tops reached the ground and they bounced and swayed in the breeze. Birch is poor-quality firewood but is better than no firewood at all, so I took my own saw and logged most of them rather than letting them go to waste. All along the edge of the wood I lined up my woodpiles, which I would leave for a year or two to season and which would make the wrens happy, offering them both hunting grounds and secure places in which to nest.

All that remained, a tangle of fallen branches, found favour with the tree pipits at least. They moved there in large numbers, with a territory around every standing tree or shrub. They would perch at the very top, then hurl themselves into the air and parachute down in their display flight. Tall spikes of purple foxgloves emerged everywhere, and then the whole site was taken over by the long pink-flowering heads of rosebay willowherb, fireweed. That first autumn after felling, when their flowers turned to seed, a breeze from the west would send vast quantities of down drifting across my front field, like a flurry of snow-flakes. Then, after the land had been left to rest a little, it was replanted, but this time with mixed hardwoods. And one day, when the spindly saplings there now have matured a little, it will grow up to be a fine, fine wood.

Penlan Cottage has a new roof now. First the well-weathered barge boards disintegrated and crashed to the ground one by one. Then the exposed beam-ends began to rot away too. Every year that went by found the cottage a little more decrepit. Everything about the cottage was original, more than a hundred and fifty years old. When the land agents came for an inspection, they thought at first that it might be enough to replace the ends of the beams and put in new eaves, but it was not to be: the damage was done, and had progressed too far. The work was overdue really, as was the replacement of the rotten window frames. The botching I had done over the years was just deferring the inevitable. All the roof timbers needed to be replaced, and the workmen also found that the entire weight of the chimney stack was resting on a rotten oak beam, so that had to be rebuilt too. I had sometimes wondered in a storm if the jackdaw ash was about to drop through my ceiling, but I had never suspected that the sudden descent of a half-ton of bricks was equally likely. The work had to be done in the middle of winter: not such a nice job for the roofers but the bat colony in the loft had to be protected from disturbance at other times of year. All the original slates, with their discs of lichen that had taken a century to grow, were replaced with perfectly even synthetic slates. My main concern was whether the bats would take to the new environment when they returned from their winter hibernation, for long-eared bats in particular are very loyal to their traditional haunts and seldom move into new locations. Most of their nursery roosts have been continuously occupied for well over a century. But I need not have worried; if anything their numbers seem to have risen a little since the new roof was put in. Perhaps the old roof was becoming a little too draughty for them as time took its toll and it gradually fell to pieces.

My cottage is not the only place that has had a revamp. The crumbling old crook barn down the hill was sold off for development, even though it was in a state of complete dilapidation and had no redeeming features whatsoever aside from the one that mattered: its location. The ancient barn was listed, so the couple who bought it had to strip it down to its bare skeleton, the exposed ribs of its original timbers, and build their home from scratch around that framework. It took them years, during which they started a family in a mobile home at the site. They said that sometimes of an evening owls would come and watch them from the fence. Tawny owls are so sedentary that these are almost certainly the distant descendants of the owl that used to shelter on the cross-beams of the old barn all those years ago when I first arrived in Wales. Now that the barn has finally been rebuilt, Penlan Cottage has a new near neighbour; still not one visible from the cottage though. Before the work had even begun, the first job that had to be done was to put in a negotiable track the half-mile or so from the lanes. A part of its route followed the old cart track along the stream, and its starting point was at the bridge where I had put my postbox. Though, sadly, my postbox was no more. The lane here was a tight zigzag, following the stream closely, sticking to the valley bottom, first following one side of the stream, then a right angle over the bridge, then another right angle to follow the stream again on its far side. Late one night someone had been driving these lanes way too fast and had lost control at the bend. They had broadsided my postbox, crushing it beyond repair, and taken out the gate, gatepost and all.

I had first moved into the cottage in the springtime, and it was in the spring a little more than five years later that I decided it was time to move on. Five years is a good long

stint at doing almost anything. I had the feeling that if I
didn't leave soon then I probably never would; I would just
stay put and spend the rest of my life there, growing old
and no doubt gradually more eccentric, alone on my hill.
This was not a prospect that in any way alarmed me; I
knew my way around this lifestyle now and staying would
have been the easy option. I had watched the turn of the
seasons over and over, and knew the worst that would be
thrown at me. I had lasted through hard droughts where
my water supply had run out and I'd had to carefully ration
water, and I had been through spells when it had rained
unremittingly, torrentially, for weeks on end. I had been
snowed in, and sat out the hardest of frosts and the wildest
of storms. I had coped with illnesses severe enough that I'd
been effectively housebound. Most of all, I had learned
that I could live a life where I did not know how long it
would be before I next had company, or even a meaningful
conversation, but could be confident that the wait would
be one not of hours or even days, but of weeks. And feel
perfectly at ease with that. When I had first moved to the
cottage, I had no idea whether I would prove capable of
tolerating a life like this, and had seen it as a challenge. But
I had long since ceased to see it in those terms. If it had ever
been a test, I had long ago torn up the exam paper and
walked out of the room; this was just me, living the life
that I had chosen.

After five years of watching the local wildlife I had
encountered just about every species I was likely to, but I
knew that there was no end to what I might see were I to
stay. It is not a matter of going somewhere and counting

off what it has to offer, as if using up its finite potential for new experience. It is more like peeling the layers from an onion, a series of reveals of deeper and deeper understanding. And some of my encounters were unique, unrepeatable moments. There would always be the possibility that something extraordinary, something totally unpredictable, might happen.

Five years is long enough to become aware not just of what stays the same – of the repeated cycles of life – but of the changes that take place over time, in yourself as well as in the world around you. Not long before I left the cottage I took one of my occasional forays to the village for supplies, following my regular route along the riverbank and the long-abandoned railway embankment. As I neared the village through that last plantation of conifers by the riverside I saw slotted tracks along the badger trail I had been following. Not an escaped lamb, I knew. When I recalled my childhood it felt like something was missing here: a party of fallow deer out in the fields at dawn, perhaps, or a pair of roe deer emerging at the edge of a woodland glade at dusk, only to dissolve back into the trees as the darkness fell. But there were no deer in this part of Wales. Until now. On my next trip to the village I looked again, and looked more carefully, and this time saw droppings too, which made me sure of what I had found. So when I had bought my few requisites from the village shop and was on my way home, I dropped by the field centre to speak to the doctor. He was not surprised; the previous day he had been driving along the lanes past these woods when a muntjac had hopped out of the plantation where I had found the

trail and run across the road in front of him – the first
record for the county. But in fact over a year earlier the
estate workers who lived by the river had been out one
evening pushing their baby buggy along the old railway
track when they had seen an unidentified mammal slipping
between two woods. Like a fox but not a fox, was how
they had described it, and with no tail. It now seemed
highly likely that this was a pioneer among the deer that
now seemed to be following the heavily wooded river valley into the heart of Wales.

The most dramatic change of all in the natural history of
the area has been the astonishing reversal in the fortunes of
the red kite. When I first moved to Penlan it must have
been a couple of weeks before I saw my first, high in the
hills over the open sheepwalk, even though this was their
heartland. In the whole of my first year at the cottage I
only twice saw one from my window. Now I think that if
you took any random skyscape viewed at any time, in any
direction, from my hillside, it would be more likely to con-
tain a kite than anything else – more likely a kite than a
buzzard or even a crow. The kites spend so much of their
lives aloft, hanging in the wind. The buzzards may be out
in force when the sun shines, but the bad weather will
ground them. Not so the kites. Their recovery has been
incremental, unstoppable, and due in good part to the
adoption of feeding stations. You can go and visit them; at
the appointed time you wait in a hide while a tractor scat-
ters butchers' offal over the field before you, turning a
whole field into a giant bird table. Overhead, the waiting
kites will be circling, a hundred or two hundred of them.

A single scan across the sky will reveal more kites than the entire British kite population those few years ago when I first moved into Penlan. There will be other birds waiting too, buzzards and ravens and magpies, but none of them has taken to this daily feeding by appointment as successfully as the kites. As the tractor that has brought the trailer full of meat scraps departs, the kites descend en masse. It is an extraordinary sight, for they do not settle to feed, but swoop and snatch with consummate grace. It is a trick they pull off extravagantly well: to look so beautiful and stylish, while feeding on carrion.

So, as the years of my stay at the cottage passed, seeing a kite sail by my window became gradually less and less remarkable, and a good walk into the mountains would almost inevitably come with several sightings. Then a pair overwintered on my hillside. That winter an hour or two's ramble around my local patch would always turn them up, even in the unusual event that they were perching. They were so big, and so conspicuous, and always seemed to choose to perch at the top of a solitary tree in full view on those infrequent occasions when they drifted down from their home in the sky. The next spring they stayed on and bred in a copse of trees high up on the steep hillside, close to the edge of the sheepwalk and looking out over miles of open air, and they have nested there ever since.

Nowadays a second pair nests lower down the hill too, their big untidy nest balanced conspicuously on an oak bough. Their chosen tree is festooned with sheeps' wool, which hangs in drapes from the branches like Spanish moss. The ranges of these two local pairs of kites seem to meet above the oaks that fringe the bottom of my front fields, so that I can see up to four of them almost continually just down the hill before me. For the most part they don't bicker and squabble like the buzzards do. This is more of a cold war; they sail up and down above the treetops as if on border patrol, facing each other off, looking but not touching, not crossing the invisible line.

But there have been less welcome changes in these hills too, most notably the gradual retreat of our moorland nesting species. It feels like a marginal habitat up there in the mountains at the best of times; it is a hard and barren place to make your home. The skylarks still call all spring – their song is the background music of the hills – but their numbers are visibly, or rather audibly, dropping, year on year. The grouse have retreated to smaller and smaller pockets where the grazing is light enough for the heather still to survive, and the whinchats seem to reduce their range a little further every year, disappearing completely from one valley at a time. Most of all I fear for our few nesting waders; we are at the southern limits of their range here and I doubt we shall have their company for much longer. The mountains will be a poorer place without the chance to stumble upon them and hear the sky ringing with their wild cries.

I spent my final week paying an almost ritual visit to some of my favourite spots, key places in the iconography of my life in the hills. Of course I spent a day by the river, down by my swimming hole, just watching the water sparkle. Always changing, but always the same. On my way there I stopped off and sat on the drystone wall looking up the flank of the mountain to the copse of cedars where the ravens had nested, every single year without fail, and were nesting still, and waited until the pair appeared, cronking and flipping on to their backs. Even after all those years, the strange optical effect that a raven has on the landscape still held the power of surprise. You look up at a mountain, and, the moment a raven appears, find yourself looking at a hill. Their seemingly unnatural bulk can make an entire landscape contract around them in an instant. My last evenings were busy: with the bats emerging from my loft and the badgers on the edge of the moor. And with the woodcock too, for of course I went down over the old stone bridge to my clearing in the woods. The character of these fields had begun to change over the years as they became more overgrown by scrub, but they still retained their magic; this was still a place that no one would find reason to visit but me.

On my last day I headed for the hills, on a full day's walk to the peatbog and back. There were two pairs of curlews calling from the black hill as usual, one at each end where the peat pools were and where the ground was soft enough for them to feed. It was a slightly overcast day and the tops felt a little bleak and lifeless as they often do. I made my way across the blasted landscape of the peatbog towards the little tarn that would be my furthest destination that day, then sat to rest on the grassy ridge that overlooked the tarn and took off my army-surplus boots and boot-socks. I stood on the brilliant – almost fluorescent – green fringe of sphagnum moss that bordered the tarn, and cold water, icy all year round, oozed between my toes. I rolled up my jeans and waded out into the red pool. A golden plover called from near by but out of sight: just one single plaintive call, the loneliest sound in the world. I didn't feel the need to go and look for it. It was enough to know that it was there.

Leftover dried foods mouse-proofed to the best of my ability. Floors mopped and dried. Beds stripped and bedding packed away. I didn't know when the cottage would next be used, though I was sure it wouldn't be long. I left just as I had arrived: with a single bag of belongings. I slammed the door shut behind me but didn't bother to lock it, though I did tie the garden gate shut with baling twine to make sure the sheep wouldn't be able to get into the garden and nibble away at the trees that I had planted. Then I headed off down the hill to the river, over the footbridge, and along my short cut to the main road, through the pine woods along the old logging trail that was becoming steadily more overgrown. I crossed the road, looked up the valley, and waited for a lift.

During the years I spent in the hills, I kept a journal. It is erratic, I wrote it only when the mood took me, and there are long gaps, as it never crossed my mind that I might one day want to make use of those notes. When I read my notebooks now I can see a dramatic change taking place from beginning to end. For the first year, it is a fairly straightforward diary, an account of where I went, what I did, and how I felt. By the second year it is strictly a nature journal: a record of my sightings and perhaps some notes on the weather. And by the third year it is virtually an almanac:

arrival dates for spring and autumn migrants; nesting records; perhaps interspersed with an occasional piece of prose capturing a fragmentary moment, say a description of the flight of a single bird. I have disappeared entirely from my own narrative; my ego has dissolved into the mist. I came to the hills to find myself, and ended up losing myself instead. And that was immeasurably better.

I live in town in England now. I see foxes here almost every night, far more than I ever saw in Wales. There are sparrowhawks aplenty here too – for those who care to look – dashing along the hedgerows between people's gardens, circling over the parks in their display flights. And from my window I can just make out the peregrine eyrie at the top of a tall tower block. But my life here is very different; sometimes I feel that I have not lived a single life but a whole series of quite distinct lives, perhaps because the change from one lifestyle to another has not been a gradual progression but the result of a snap decision here, a sudden switching of tracks there.

I try to visit the cottage as often as I can, engineering my life so that at least once or twice a year I can make it to Penlan alone for a while. Of course this is a very different experience from that of the years when I had no other life, in the same way that a short package holiday is different from the open-ended travels of my youth, when I just kept going, on and on, until I ran out of money, or health, or inclination. But there is a curious thing that happens to me on these visits. For the first hour or two, I race around, checking the slates on the roof, bringing in firewood and lighting the fire, filling the lamps, unpacking the food I have brought, making up my bed. And then at some point I sit down in the old wicker armchair in front of the log fire, put my feet up and forget myself. It is as if there is a switch in my mind that takes me back in time. All the intervening years just fall away and are gone, and it is as though I had never left.